In a Heartbeat

In a Heartbeat

SHARING THE POWER *of* CHEERFUL GIVING

Leigh Anne AND
Sean Tuohy

WITH Sally Jenkins

Henry Holt and Company
New York

Henry Holt and Company, LLC
Publishers since 1866
175 Fifth Avenue
New York, New York 10010
www.henryholt.com

Henry Holt® and ® are registered trademarks of Henry Holt and Company, LLC.

Library of Congress Cataloging-in-Publication Data

Tuohy, Leigh Anne.
    In a heartbeat : sharing the power of cheerful giving / Leigh Anne and Sean
Tuohy with Sally Jenkins.—1st ed.
        p. cm.
    ISBN 978-0-312-57718-6
    1. Adoptive parents—United States—Biography.   2. Tuohy, Leigh Anne.
3. Tuohy, Sean.   4. Generosity.   5. Social action.   6. Oher, Michael.
7. Football players—United States.   I. Tuohy, Sean.   II. Jenkins, Sally.
III. Title.
    HV874.8.T84 2010
    362.734092'273—dc22
    [B]   2010017545

Henry Holt books are available for special promotions and premiums.
For details contact: Director, Special Markets.

First Edition 2010

Designed by Meryl Sussman Levavi

For all the children fighting to survive
in the invisible cracks of our society, we see you.

No one has ever become poor by giving.

—ANNE FRANK

Contents

Prologue: The Popcorn Theory (LEIGH ANNE AND SEAN)   1

1. Getting (SEAN)   28

    INTERLUDE ✦ Tim McGraw (ACTOR)   61

2. Giving (LEIGH ANNE)   64

    INTERLUDE ✦ Sandra Bullock (ACTRESS)   96

3. The Two-Penny Gift (LEIGH ANNE AND SEAN)   100

    INTERLUDE ✦ Collins Tuohy (DAUGHTER)   140

4. Passing It On (LEIGH ANNE AND SEAN)   143

    INTERLUDE ✦ Michael Oher (SON)   181

5. Giving and Getting (LEIGH ANNE AND SEAN)   184

    INTERLUDE ✦ Sean Junior (SON)   225

6. Blindsided (LEIGH ANNE AND SEAN)   230

How You Can Help   265

Acknowledgments   267

In a Heartbeat

Prologue

The Popcorn Theory

LEIGH ANNE AND SEAN

*We all begin on the same page and we're all going to
end on the same page.*

—SEAN TUOHY

AFTER MANY YEARS OF GETTING AND SPENDING, OF
being broke, then rich, then almost broke again, of cashing in
and paying up, and—let's face it—hoping to die with the
most toys, we're convinced that it's better to give than receive.
Some folks call that philanthropy. But we aren't the fancy
types. We don't always have enough starch in our shirts and
our household is about as formal as a sandbox. Instead, we
live by a more informal notion, which we call the Popcorn
Theory.

It goes like this: "You can't help everyone. But you can try
to help the hot ones who pop right up in front of your face."

The Popcorn Theory is about noticing others. It starts

with recognizing a fellow soul by the roadside as kindred, even if he doesn't seem to belong in your gated community and, at six foot five and over three hundred pounds, is the biggest piece of popcorn you ever saw. It's about acknowledging that person's potential and value. It's about seeing him, instead of looking past him.

"Like with popcorn, you don't know which kernel's gonna pop," Sean likes to say. "But the hot ones just show up. It's not hard to spot 'em."

Except, that first day we almost drove right by him.

It was a raw autumn morning in late November 2002, the day before Thanksgiving. A light dusting of snow had just fallen, which we in Memphis, Tennessee—being Southerners—considered a blizzard. Ice draped the roof gutters and the sky was dull and blanched, a waste-colored day.

We were on our way out to breakfast. He was trudging down the street in nothing but a T-shirt and shorts, his arms wrapped in a sad knot, his breath visible in the cold.

We glanced at him, briefly. Then we did what comes too easily to all of us. To be honest—gut-punch honest—we kept on driving and passed him by. Past the occasional patches of snow that lay on the yards like sheets half pulled back. Past the stubbled lawns and the freeze-cracked sidewalks.

But, as we left him behind, a thought tugged at Leigh Anne's consciousness. It was as faint as the wind, as indistinct as the chittering of birds.

"Turn around," Leigh Anne said.

With that, our lives changed in a heartbeat.

❧

If you are among the millions of people who saw the movie *The Blind Side*, or read the book it was based on, then you know what happened next. You know how a wealthy suburban couple pulled over and spoke to young, rootless Michael Oher. How Michael was a ward of the state, his mother an addict, his father murdered. How he ran away from twenty foster homes and passed through eleven schools before he met us. How he eventually became a second son to us and earned a football scholarship to the University of Mississippi, where he made the Chancellor's Honor Roll. How he then went on to stardom in the National Football League. How an Academy Award–nominated film was made about our family, and how Sandra Bullock won her first Oscar for her portrayal of Leigh Anne.

You probably think you know everything about us, our whole story. Actually, you only know part of it. Don't get us wrong. Our friend Michael Lewis, the author of *The Blind Side*, wrote a wonderful book that deserved to be a bestseller. (Most of his books sell big. We haven't read all of them, but if you see him, tell him we did.) Our friend Sandra Bullock is a brilliant actress and her star turn in the movie, all nerve and bluntness, was perfect. (Leigh Anne doesn't actually wear skirts that tight, but it's a minor point.) Compared to our real lives, though, the book and movie were just sketches.

For instance, people ask all the time: "Is Leigh Anne Tuohy really like that?"

Our friends are quick to answer: "It's worse. The movie could only get an hour and a half of her in."

The truth is, childbirth is easier to explain than our story. So in this book we'd like to introduce our family properly, tell you how we saw events through our own eyes, and deliver our message in our own voices.

It's a message about giving. We often say that our son Michael gave us much more than we gave him. That confuses people: how is it possible that a homeless kid could give anything to wealthy parents who already had two perfect children? It's possible because in every exchange with Michael, we came out on the better end. We gave him a home—and he gave us back a stronger and more centered family. We gave him advice and support—and he gave us back a deeper awareness of the world. We gave him love as a boy—and he gave us back a man to be proud of. Each thing we gave to him has been returned to us multiplied.

But before any of that could happen, something else had to happen first. A fundamental precondition had to be met.

We had to notice him. We had to *see* him.

☙

At this point we should pause to explain why a couple of well-heeled suburbanites would go *out* to breakfast on a weekday morning. The answer is that we don't cook. Or, to be more specific, Leigh Anne doesn't cook. As Sean likes to tell people, "My wife believes that if somebody else cooked it, and we bring it home and eat it, that's 'home cooking.'"

Our son Sean Junior, who we call S.J. for short, claims that our conversations about meals always consist of the following exchange:

"What's for dinner?"

"Whatever you pick up."

S.J. also likes to tell the story of our Kroger's supermarket card. A while back the local grocery started a program: for every fifty bucks spent at Kroger's, four dollars would go to the school or charity of your choice. After about a year, our grand contribution to the team, based on the amount of food we purchased, came to just seven dollars. The only things we ever bought were Diet Coke and Gatorade.

Actually, we almost didn't even have a kitchen in our house. Several years ago we moved into a lovely home in the upper-crust River Oaks section of Memphis, thanks to our dual success in business—Leigh Anne as an interior designer, Sean as an entrepreneur in the fast-food business. Due to the growth of Leigh Anne's firm, Flair I Interiors, and Sean's company, RGT Management—which over the years has acquired more than eighty Taco Bells, Pizza Huts, and Long John Silver's—we were fortunate enough to be able to buy and remodel a beautiful four-bedroom, cream-brick manor on a bucolic street called Shady Grove Lane.

Leigh Anne handled the remodeling discussions with the architect, who then drew up some plans. When she showed the blueprints to the rest of the family, we all stared at them for a long moment.

"Where's the kitchen?" Sean said to Leigh Anne.

Meaningful pause.

"I don't plan on cooking."

Longer pause.

"All right," Sean replied patiently, "let's approach this from the practical side. What if we ever want to sell the house? Who would buy a house with no kitchen?"

Stubborn, emphatic pause.

"I don't plan on selling the house."

Eventually, we struck a compromise: a small passageway lined with bookshelves was converted into a galley kitchen. Sean likes to show it off to visitors by spreading his arms out in the tiny space. "See this?" he'll say. "This was a *negotiation*."

Even now, it's immaculate because it's so seldom used. As our daughter, Collins, tells her friends, "It's like a hospital operating room."

S.J. enjoys throwing open the refrigerator door to show visitors what's inside: nothing but bottles. We have drinks. We have sauces. We have condiments, ketchup, and mustard. We have seasonings, stuff to put *on* food. But no actual food.

By now you may have gathered that our family is a little . . . odd.

So that's why we were out driving that morning. We were on our way to get some home cooking.

❦

That day in the car when we spotted Michael, ambling slowly along a tidy cement walk and past a series of wrought iron gates behind which peeked the tall gables of grand homes, we each had the same fleeting thought. We wondered, inwardly, what a black kid was doing in that neighborhood at nine thirty in the morning. Frankly, he was out of place. In that part of town, it's a little unusual to see someone walking on foot, much less a very tall, very large, dark-complexioned person in shorts.

"He looks like a fish out of water," Leigh Anne said aloud, peering through the windshield.

Memphis, of course, has a long and tortured racial history. But if you live in River Oaks—a stately, wholly white enclave—it's easy to avert your eyes from the city's race and class divisions, or ignore them altogether. Thick-chimneyed Mock Tudors and faux French chateaus are tucked behind whitewashed brick walls. The subdivisions have European names like Normandy Court and they exude affluence and seclusion. They are sheltered by old oaks and pines and heavy hedges and protected by thick garden walls. There's no concertina wire, but you get the idea.

As we passed Michael, Sean recognized him. He was the "new kid" everyone was talking about at Briarcrest Christian School.

The pleasant, redbrick high school where we sent our children was just four blocks from our house. Briarcrest had been founded in 1973 as a response to the court-ordered racial integration of the Memphis City Schools, when the flight of white parents had resulted in a burgeoning of small, private, reassuringly homogenous halls of education. Most of the kids at Briarcrest came from the same neighborhoods and their families enjoyed the same income levels.

But, to its credit, Briarcrest had begun to seek out and admit minority children, partly out of a philanthropic impulse, partly in the interest of giving its affluent students fuller exposure to the actual world around them. Michael was one of these minority kids—he'd only just arrived and he stuck out like a sore thumb.

As it happens, Michael was the same age and in the same class as our daughter, Collins. One day she had encountered him on the staircase on her way to anatomy. He was going up and she was going down, and he took up the entire passageway. She had to back up so he could get past her. She remembers thinking, "That's the largest person I've ever seen."

The next day she introduced herself to him. He just said, "Hey." She didn't get many words out of him in their first few encounters.

Sean had also noticed him at Briarcrest, where he volunteered in the afternoons as a basketball coach. It was his habit to drop by the school during his lunch break and he had spotted Michael in the gym, sitting in the bleachers watching some kids play ball. One afternoon Sean spoke with Michael briefly, and he came home talking about the huge new kid who had great hands and feet to go along with his size. Sean saw right away that Michael might be a real asset to the Briarcrest athletic teams.

As we left Michael in the rearview mirror that November morning, the two of us had a brief conversation.

"That's the new kid at Briarcrest I told you about," Sean said.

"What's he doing out here this time of day?" Leigh Anne asked. "School's not in session."

"I don't know."

And that was it. No question about it, we intended to keep driving. We were more concerned with breakfast. Actually, we were preoccupied with food in general, given that it was the day before Thanksgiving. We wouldn't be cooking ourselves, of course, but the previous evening we had spent a couple of hours helping Leigh Anne's mother—who would be hosting the family meal extravaganza—dice and chop.

Later on, we learned that Thanksgiving didn't mean much to Michael. Neither did Christmas, or his birthday. These days weren't for celebrating, quite the opposite. They were bleak, neutral days that only reminded him of want. "I went through a lot of those days with nothing," he told us. "A holiday was just another date to me."

We glided down the street in our BMW, a plush and comfortable silver cloud, fine with the world. But then it began to sleet, and that's when the thought whispered to Leigh Anne.

Why doesn't he have long pants on in November?

The thought grew until it forced itself into her throat and demanded to be spoken aloud.

"Turn around."

"What? Why?"

"Go back and let's see what he's doing here."

"Maybe he's going to the school."

"That's all fine, Sean, but why does he only have a T-shirt and shorts on in this weather?"

"I don't have a clue."

"TURN AROUND."

Anyone who has heard Leigh Anne Tuohy speak in that tone invariably does what he is told. Sean promptly U-turned the car right in the middle of the street, as ordered.

One of the things Mister Tuohy understands after twenty-eight years of marriage is how not to aggravate Missus Tuohy. Another thing he understands is how aggressive she is when a kid has needs—aggressive being a polite term for borderline obnoxious. Kids drive her crazy, because whatever is wrong in their lives is not their fault. Just by looking at Michael, Leigh Anne could tell that he had never hurt a soul. And he was shivering.

We pulled up beside him and Sean rolled down the driver's side window with an electric hum.

"Hey, Michael, what are you doing over here today?"

Slowly, Michael folded himself in half and bent down to the window. His expression was placid, gentle eyed. His voice when he spoke was mellow, deep chested, and surprisingly beautiful. He had a voice like a cello.

"I'm going to shoot hoops."

"Well, the gym's not open."

To Leigh Anne, leaning across from the passenger seat, it was immediately apparent that Michael was disappointed. He had an "Oh, no" kind of look. It was obvious to her that he now had no mission, no plan—and no place else to go.

"They got heat there," Michael said uncertainly.

He was going to the school because it was warm.

"Let us take you home," Leigh Anne said.

"Oh, no, no, no," he replied, with something like alarm. "I'm okay, I don't need anything."

"Well," said Leigh Anne, "why don't you at least let us take you back up to the bus stop where you got off. When does another express come by?"

"I don't know," he said.

After another minute of conversation, Michael clearly realized how persistent Leigh Anne intended to be. We simply weren't going to leave him standing there in the sleet in a T-shirt. Finally, he agreed to let us drive him to another bus stop and he climbed in the car.

There was hardly any talk as we drove. A little basketball chitchat, nothing more. What was going through our heads? Not much. All these years later, Leigh Anne is the only one of us who can recall having a specific thought that day. The first thing she thought was, "This kid needs some clothes." It was apparent that he didn't own any cold-weather garments. Next, she thought, "I wonder who would know what size he wears?" But she couldn't bring herself to ask him any questions. We didn't know anything about him or his life and we didn't want to patronize him.

We arrived at the bus stop and let Michael out. He waved good-bye. That was it, the end of the first encounter. It was nothing, and everything.

❦

The following Monday, when school was back in session, Leigh Anne went over to Briarcrest and began asking some questions. Who was this kid? Where did he live? Where were his parents?

No one had any firm answers. The counselors knew next to nothing about him, except that he had been brought to the school in September by a youth basketball coach named Tony Henderson, with whom he had spent a few nights. Henderson had persuaded the Briarcrest administration to enroll Michael as a hardship case, on academic probation.

Leigh Anne dropped by the gym and queried Briarcrest basketball coach John Harrington, who said, "I don't know that much about him yet, but I do think he probably is lacking in clothes." Leigh Anne said, "Will you ask him if he will let me take him shopping?" John said he would approach Michael and let us know. That night John called Leigh Anne to say that Michael had agreed to let her buy him some things.

The next day, as Michael climbed into the car after basketball practice, Leigh Anne began to grapple with the scale of his potential needs. For starters, he was such a big kid that she had no idea where to look for sizes that would fit him.

Surveying him, she said, "Okay. Where are we going? Do you know where we could get you some clothes?"

Michael looked back at her with an impatient, adolescent expression, like she'd just said something stupid. He sort of snorted, "Yeahhh."

"Well, I certainly can't take you to Macy's," she shot back, "so point me in the right direction."

That was the first small seed of a rapport and it grew from there. In the months ahead, our relationship with Michael would develop with a lot of sarcastic back-and-forth, and a lot of teasing, which was what we did in our home. Michael learned pretty quickly that in the Tuohy household you can say just about anything and not get in trouble.

In the weeks that followed, Michael began spending more and more time hanging around the house. But he wasn't the only one. We had supported and cared for plenty of kids besides Michael. (We still do.) A lot of them were athletes looking for a way up and out through sports, kids who were on the margin financially or academically. We had a natural sympathy for them; earlier in our lives, as we will explain, we had had much less ourselves. Besides Michael, there was a boy in the band and a young girl on the softball team. We wanted our home to be open to them and to all of our children's friends. Our house was like a hive: kids came over to share our takeout, or to be tutored by Sean, or just to play video games with S.J. Michael was different only in that he had greater needs. Truth be told, he needed more than any kid we had ever met.

But if there is a fundamental misapprehension about Michael, it's that he needed saving. As we got to know him during those first few weeks, we discovered that underneath his shyness, his foot shuffling, and his head ducking, he had a tremendous will to determine the course of his own life. If he initially seemed forlorn, and searching, that was because he felt guarded and out of place because of what he'd been through. But buried under his skin, like rock under soil, was a deep confidence, a sense of his own capacities. You saw flashes of it when he would cut his eyes up at you and smile. In that instant, you could see all that he had inside of him, as if the landscape of his mind had just been lit up by lightning.

Eventually, we came to understand that Michael was almost always the smartest person in the room. It just took a while for all of us to realize it. If anything, he was almost too sharp for his own good. As Sean would sometimes joke, "He thinks he could perform surgery with a butter knife." Miss Sue Mitchell, his academic tutor in high school and college, once said, "If Michael and I are ever in a car wreck together, please do not let him operate on me. Because he thinks he can."

The point is, Michael was always going to find a way to make it out of his situation—and nobody was going to be more responsible for his success than he was. He knew what he wanted and he found ways to attain it. "I knew there had to be something better," he said later. "I'd say, 'Man, there has to be something else. I just have to better myself.'"

Michael came to us this great, sweet, bright kid, ready-made for success. All we did was give him a few tools and step out of the way. We allowed him to become who he was supposed to be. He was such a self-made man, in fact, that when he later saw the portrayal of himself as a boy in the movie, he said, "I was never like that." He didn't like seeing himself as he was. He argued that he never had trouble meeting people and looking them in the eye, and he all but insisted that he was born with a 3.5 grade point average. To him, none of his past happened. What he is *now* is what happened. Sometimes we argue with him—in all honesty, it's still hard for us to know how to treat his past—but then we let it go. His childhood is his own property. He would probably not be the success he is without the ability to transcend his past. He simply refuses to let it catch his sleeve and drag him backward.

⚘

A couple of weeks after we picked Michael up and took him to the bus stop, he spent the night on our couch for the first time. At that point he was drifting from household to household, dividing his nights between three or four different families from Briarcrest. He occasionally spent nights with a young assistant football coach named Matt Saunders. He also spent a lot of nights with a classmate named Quinterio Franklin, who lived out in Mississippi about thirty-five miles away.

When Michael stayed with us, he slept on a sofa in our game room, a broad, many-windowed space that reflects the Tuohy love of toys. It's got three different flat-screen TVs, a Pop-A-Shot basketball machine, an Xbox rig, and a view of the swimming pool outside. It's also got a large L-shaped sectional couch.

The running family joke is that Leigh Anne took Michael into her heart the first time she saw how neatly he folded everything. He treated that sofa as if it were the property of the U.S. military. After his first night with us, we all stared at the blanket folded and cornered in a neat bundle and at the sheets he had so crisply squared.

"Instant love," S.J. remarked.

No one else in the household would have done such a thing. Except for Leigh Anne, of course. The rest of us are all wrecks—which is why we need her.

Collins's room during high school was so messy that it drove Leigh Anne to distraction. Collins lived in piles. You could see the Monday pile, the Tuesday pile, and the Wednesday pile. There was the formal-wear pile and the semiformal pile. Leigh Anne would take videos of the room and show it to visitors, in hopes of embarrassing Collins into cleaning up the mess. When that didn't work, Leigh Anne would scream, "I'm going to throw her out of the house!" Finally, Collins would clean her room . . . and a couple days later, you'd see the piles on the floor again.

For all the chaos and yelling, it was apparent to any outsider who walked into the Tuohy household that we were a close family—if a functionally dysfunctional one. We didn't come home to the smell of fresh-cooked meals every night but we laughed a lot. We didn't have many Dr. Phil moments, either. We were moving too fast. Our lives were simply too hectic—who's got time for serious conflict?

Michael's first impressions of the cast of characters in our house were pretty vivid. Here's what he saw in each of us.

Leigh Anne: a former cheerleader, and five foot two of plainspoken will. She wanted to get things done and usually what she wanted to get done needed doing. If anyone tried to stop her, she'd take his arm off and walk down the street with it. She had a shiny exterior, glittering and bejeweled, that covered for tenderness. She cried on Sunday at Grace Evangelical Church when Pastor Jimmy Young read her mother's favorite scriptures or called for her father's favorite hymn, "Up from the Grave He Rose." But that didn't mean you wanted to mess with her.

"I'm all about loving and giving," Leigh Anne would say, "but I'm going to kick your butt if you do something you're not supposed to do."

Sean: gently sarcastic in tone and in manner, he pretended to be the minority partner. "I get a 49 percent vote," he'd say. In reality, he was probably the strongest person in the family. Sometimes others in the family seemed almost to ignore him, but when there was a crisis, everybody ran right to him. He oversaw dozens of fast-food franchises and he was also a broadcaster for the Memphis Grizzlies, the local NBA team. He was short on time and big on results. He refused to read the instructions to anything—he just went from A to D and didn't want to know what steps B and C were.

Collins: picture a luminous changeling with waist-length hair—and biceps. Collins—or Collie-Bell, as others in the family liked to call her—managed to be all things at once, gorgeous and athletic, sweet and a smarty-pants. She was the member of the family to whom everything came effortlessly. Before Michael arrived she was the best athlete in the house. She would master a sport, become bored, and move on. She was a gymnastics prodigy and later one of the best swimmers in the city. She triple-jumped and then won a state championship in the pole vault.

Sean Junior: An antic child, with a thick slab of black hair falling over his eyes and speech that came all in a rush. Of everyone in the family, he was the most perceptive and attuned to others. He had a strange, hyperkinetic mind; he was a king of the universe at Xbox, and he made straight As though he hardly cracked a book. Somehow, against all odds, he was also self-assured. The youngest in a frenzied household, he was always being left behind but never seemed to mind it. His good humor was bottomless. When he played basketball for a local boys club team that was made up completely of black kids, except for him, his teammates nicknamed him "Spot."

The family came and went at all hours and seemed to live completely in the moment. Sean would need five clean suits for a road trip because in addition to overseeing his restaurants, he was traveling all over the country doing his broadcasting for the Grizzlies. Collins couldn't find her pole vault gear in all the piles, Leigh Anne was juggling decorating jobs, and S.J. needed a ride somewhere. The merry-go-round never stopped—or even slowed down.

Then Michael came along. It didn't take long for him to understand what we were all saying to him: "If you want to jump into this frying pan with us, let's go!"

✿

There was never a moment when Michael formally joined our family. It just happened. Monday became Tuesday and Tuesday became Wednesday. He'd stop by the house to hang out between classes and practices, which became hanging out to study, which became spending the night, which became staying for three nights, which became staying for a month. All of a sudden six months had gone by. At some point we realized that Michael had been living with us for a long time. It just evolved into what it was.

At first we were just too busy to stop and think about what was happening. It was only later that we understood that a mutual awakening had taken place and began to measure the size of the awkward gaps we confronted, between privileged and poor, between black and white. And only then did we begin to bridge these gaps as a family.

One of the questions we're asked most frequently is, how were Collins, S.J., and Michael able to accept one another as brothers and sister without resentment? We're not exactly sure, except that they were born good-natured, and we didn't ruin them. For some reason, our three kids aren't sitting on some psychiatrist's couch saying, "I got screwed." How did that happen? We don't know. But we do know that the three of them cared for each other as much as anybody.

One possible answer is that we all laughed a lot. Another is that Collins and S.J. were open to Michael because they hadn't been raised in total privilege and prosperity. When they were younger, they saw us struggle economically, so they grew up with some sense for how hard we worked and how fortunate they were. We also tried hard not to sequester them socially—because when you're socially sequestered, you're susceptible to stereotypes and to viewing a lot of people as "others." We never wanted our kids to view anyone as an "other."

Not long before we met Michael, we sent Collins to a program called Bridge Builders. It's a weeklong seminar during which schoolchildren from the dead opposite ends of the city are placed in dormitory rooms on the University of Memphis campus and required to get to know each other. The program is run by a Memphis nonprofit foundation called Bridges, which for eighty years has been fostering racial and social justice through a variety of community initiatives. They mentor local "peacemakers" and help young dropouts get their equivalency degrees and find jobs. "Changing Memphis One Life at a Time" is the program's slogan.

For five days, Collins—who was then a sophomore in high school—roomed with a girl from Raleigh-Egypt High School on the other side of town. Raleigh-Egypt was the opposite of Briarcrest socially and economically; it had a mixed student body and its share of problems. On one occasion, for instance, a student had slapped a teacher.

None of the kids in the program were allowed to use cell phones except in an emergency. Communication with friends on the outside was strictly forbidden, so all the kids had was each other. Through a series of encounters and counselor-led seminars, Bridge Builders knocked down social barriers and forced the kids to lean on one another. At first Collins and her roommate were all about checking out each other's hair. But as they got better acquainted, they discovered they were separated by—and curious about—some of the simplest things.

One exercise in particular made a lasting impression on Collins. A counselor gathered about fifteen or twenty kids together in a room, lined them up single-file, and turned out the lights. In the dark, the counselor asked them to close their eyes and listen to a series of questions. The students were to respond to the questions simply by taking a step to the left or right. If the answer to the question was yes, they were to step to the right. If the answer was no, they had to step to the left.

"Are you going to get a car when you're sixteen?"

Collins heard shuffling in the dark. She took a step to the right.

"Do your parents have jobs?"

More shuffling. Collins took another step to the right.

"Do you have two parents?"

Still more shuffling. Collins again moved to the right.

After a few more questions, the counselor said, "Open your eyes."

The lights flickered on.

Collins stared around the room. Almost all of the kids were on opposite sides of the room. They had been pushed to either one wall or the other by their family's circumstances. Just a few kids stood in the center.

Collins thought, "So this is why we're the way we are."

⚘

If the message you take from our experience is that a rich white family tried to save a black kid, then you will totally miss our story's meaning. It has nothing to do with where we were from, how we lived, or how much money we had. It's not important what color we were, whether we had glasses or didn't have glasses, or what kind of shoes we wore. All of that is irrelevant. Some people have tried to make it relevant—but they emphasize the wrong thing.

It so happened that when we first met him, Michael was a black, sixteen-year-old male. But those words are just adjectives that describe the person we tried to help and ultimately came to love. Making him a part of the family was an unconscious act, and it happened in a heartbeat.

It's equally true, however, that the outlook on life that allowed us to open our hearts and home to Michael was developed over the course of our lifetimes. If the impulse was sudden, the two of us had been thinking for several years about our philosophy of giving.

One of our deepest beliefs is beautifully captured in the Second Epistle of Paul to the Corinthians, or 2 Corinthians. The seventh verse of the ninth chapter of 2 Corinthians reads: "Each one must give as he has decided in his heart, not reluctantly or under compulsion, for God loves a cheerful giver." After many years of attending church together, and helping to found one of the fastest-growing congregations in Memphis, Grace Evangelical, we came to believe that a cheerful, spontaneous offering, no matter how small, could be increased and made powerful by God. Our faith helped us understand that it was up to us to be generous and make ourselves available to be used by others.

We also became convinced that in order to really give, we had to get our hearts right. We had to learn that it was important to let go of any particular agenda. What were we hoping to achieve when we gave? We knew that it couldn't be "We're looking to go out and help a fourteen-year-old Hispanic boy today."

So many people we knew wanted to make a difference and yet they waited for a really important cause to come along. Or they waited for their big bonus check to come in. They said to themselves: "I want to save Africa." Or: "I want to save the American Indian." They had an agenda. But why is it necessary to have an agenda? Because it relieves our conscience? Or makes us look good to our bosses? Or makes us feel good about ourselves? Because it makes us more appealing to the congregation? Or gives us more points on our Visa card? Or means that the United Way is going to give us a plaque?

The more we thought about the nature of true charity, the more we realized that there's a paradox in Americans' general attitudes toward giving: as a citizenry we are at once charitable and stingy. According to the National Philanthropic Trust, 89 percent of American households give to charity. Sounds impressive, but think about this: on average, we donate just 1.9 percent of our household income. To be frank, that's miserly. Especially considering how enriched some of us are, that percentage is well below what it should be. And by biblical standards—as most Christians would undoubtedly agree—it's downright shameful.

As we reflected on our own ways of giving, we came to see that we often approached charity too formally. Giving shouldn't always be a prescribed ritual or ceremony; it doesn't need to be accompanied by properly stamped paperwork. If we worried less about the procedures and methods of giving and concentrated more on a giving state of mind, we might have more to offer than we knew.

It pained us to realize that we too often failed at the simplest kind of giving. While we were waiting for a great cause, or focused on an agenda, we chose not to notice someone standing right in front of us. We looked right past the woman in the grocery store taking things out of her basket because she was short on cash or the elderly disabled man in line at CVS.

Ultimately, we agreed that by embracing a smaller and more cheerful kind of giving, we might ease a lot of everyday problems. It took several years but slowly, informally, we found ourselves arriving at a simple conclusion: it wasn't important to do something great.

Instead, we decided to take this approach: do small things with great love. If we could do that, little opportunities to give might grow beyond our wildest dreams.

And that's exactly what happened when Michael walked into our lives. We didn't set out to take in a homeless kid. We just gave him a ride. He was the ultimate example of the Popcorn Theory.

Too often we think we lack the means to improve someone's lot. We're wrong. The Popcorn Theory doesn't oblige all of us to write impressively large checks or take in every hungry child with a face like a flame. It only requires that we perceive the person standing right in front of us.

⚜

Not long ago we heard the following story from a U.S. senator we met during a trip to Washington for an Adoption Coalition convention. There is a little-known congressional program that awards internships to young people who have aged out of the foster care system. These are kids who were never adopted and are no longer eligible for state support. They have no families and few prospects. The internship program is a way to give a few of them a decent professional start.

This senator we met during the convention employed one such young man as an intern. One morning the senator breezed in for a meeting and discovered that his intern was already in the office, reorganizing the entire mailroom. The senator said to the intern, "This is amazing—the mailroom has never looked so clean. You did a great job."

A few minutes later the senator decided to get a cup of coffee. As he passed by the mailroom, he glanced through the plate-glass window and saw that the intern had tears streaming down his face. The senator stopped short, wondering what could have upset him.

He returned to the mailroom and said, "Son, are you okay?"

"Yes," the intern answered quietly, wiping his tears away.

"Did I say something to offend you?"

"No, sir."

"Well, what's wrong?"

After a short silence, the young man said, "That's the first time in my life anyone's told me that I did something good."

A bit of attention and a kind word—that's how little it takes to affect someone's life for the better.

❧

Thousands of people failed to notice Michael Oher, his quality and his promise. Every day, as he walked the long blocks from the bus stop to school, they drove right past him. Now, Michael was hard to miss. But nobody seemed to have noticed him. Nobody ever stopped to ask, "Where are you going?" Nobody even offered him a ride.

After we met Michael, we became very conscious of his old bus stop. Leigh Anne is a power walker who does five miles a day and, from that Thanksgiving on, whenever she strode up to that bus stop she always took note of the people who were waiting for a bus and stopped to speak to them. Sometimes she just said, "How is your day?" Or she paused to ask a few questions and find out more about them. There was an orthopedic clinic nearby and some of them were on their way to get medical care. (We never even knew the clinic was there.) Others were on their way to work at a Chick-fil-A on the nearby commercial strip. (We'd never thought about how they got to work.) Most of them were taken aback when Leigh Anne stopped for conversation. They got a look on their faces that said, "People don't usually talk to me in this part of town."

Try an experiment. At some point in the next twenty-four hours you're going to come across someone who seems of no consequence. Ask yourself if you see value in this person. It might be a young woman in a restaurant clearing off the tables. It might be the young man who parks your car in a garage. It might be someone standing on the curb at a red light or waiting at a bus stop. Pay attention to how you respond. You will glance at them, barely, and you will place some type of value on them. (You're lying if you say you don't.) You will pass right by them and if you give them a second thought, it will be this: you're better than they are.

By the time Michael was seventeen or eighteen, he might have completely fallen through the cracks, unnoticed by anyone. After all, who cared where Michael slept, what he ate, what he wore, or where he went? To be brutal about it, who really cared whether he lived or died?

Even after Michael made it to the NFL, people still didn't seem to value him, to *see* him, as clearly as they should have. For instance, when Sandra Bullock went on the *Late Show with David Letterman*, she had an exchange with Letterman that struck all of us. No doubt he didn't mean anything by it, but Letterman kept referring to "that boy in the movie." You could tell it got to Sandra. She finally said, "You mean *Michael*."

To us, the astonishing commercial success of *The Blind Side* is rooted in a kind of self-examination. Michael's story causes all of us to search our souls and it shows us how we too easily ignore, debase, and devalue each other. The experience of watching the movie is kind of like hearing a sermon when you've screwed up and suddenly the sermon seems directed right at you. But the movie also touches the part of us that wants to be better, that yearns to treat each other as family. The story it tells is a reaffirmation of the way we *want* to feel about who we are and the way we want our country to be.

We're often asked, wasn't it a risk to take Michael into your home? You know what? You take a bigger risk every day of your life. When you get in your car and drive across a bridge, you take a risk. You don't know if your tires are going to blow out, or if the bridge's pilings are going to hold up, or if there's a drunk driver coming at you from the other end of the bridge. But you don't stop and think about it, do you? You don't get up every morning and kick each of your tires. You don't stare at the bridge and say, "Yeah, I think it'll hold me." You go right ahead and cross that bridge without giving it a thought.

Everybody takes risks, every day. You just don't realize that's what you're doing. For us, loving Michael was like that. We just crossed the bridge without thinking about it. And the way we see it, these are the kinds of risks that all of us need to take more of.

This is not to say that we don't have problems or make mistakes. It's not like we give everything away and go around wearing sackcloth, either. Like most people, we spend too much money on too many things, from golf clubs to David Yurman earrings. All you have to do is take a look at Collins's Louis Vuitton MacBook cover—Michael bought it for her—or check out the four cars in our garage, including young S.J.'s Dodge Challenger—Michael bought it for him—to know that.

Moreover, we're the first to admit that we weren't always

the most generous givers ourselves and also that our views about giving were strongly influenced by others, starting with our parents. In the chapters to come, we'll show you how giving was passed down as a legacy to us and how we're trying to pass it to our children.

As you'll see, we have our flaws. You could even say that we have major issues. But, in the end, we're like every family. We have our disagreements and our insensitivities. We don't always like how other members of the family behave. We fight. We make up. And we get over it.

That's what families do.

1

Getting

SEAN

*Character is something that you cannot buy, and it's
something that cannot be taken from you. You can
only lose it. It's the most important thing you own.*

—SEAN TUOHY

I DON'T KNOW WHO WON THE WAR OF 1812 AND I'M
not real sure how to outline the Pythagorean theorem, but I'm
good with two things: money and kids. I can relate to any part
of a kid's life if they are poor, because growing up I was closer
to poor than rich. When someone says to me, "There goes a
scholarship kid," with a tone that suggests pity or condescen-
sion, I answer, "*I* was a scholarship kid. That was me."

Poverty equates to failure—that's the way we look at it in
America. We congratulate those who overcome their meager
backgrounds but then we point the finger at someone else and
say, "Why can't *you*?" The fact is, not every kid can overcome it.
Some kids do, some kids don't. When you have to worry about

sleeping, eating, lights, heat—those kinds of things—it's harder. I say that from a certain amount of personal experience. I say it as someone who had to hustle lunches by winning bets.

It's easy to beat a kid up. The hard thing is to build him up.

I learned that from my dad, Ed "Skeets" Tuohy. My father was a legendary high school basketball coach in New Orleans, which is where I'm from. My parents struggled to raise four children on the extremely modest salary of a gym teacher. Yet Dad dealt with financial pressure the way he did everything else, with wit and composure. He believed nothing was too serious to be laughed at, an inherited trait. He had the unconcerned humor of an Irishman whose family immigrated to Chicago's South Side.

Dad joked that he would pay our bills by lottery. Some creditor would call and say, "You haven't paid your bill."

He'd reply, "Sorry! You didn't win the lottery."

"What do you mean by that?"

"Well, I put all the bills in a hat and pulled out three, and you weren't one of them."

We lived in a tiny shotgun house wedged between the grander homes of the city's Uptown district. It was a modest little place in an immodest neighborhood, with six of us crammed into four bedrooms. We had just one bathroom, and we were always on top of one another—it was nothing for three of us to do our bathing rituals at the same time.

Breakfast every morning was a single poached egg that my mom, Mida, cooked with a lot of love. But I got to hating the meal so much I would feed it to the whippet that lived next door. After a couple of years the dog died; my older brother and I were always afraid the cholesterol got him.

I spent my childhood figuring out how to make a living in the land of the rich. The only silver spoon I ever had was the one I stole from my kindergarten classmate, Michael Lewis. I worked a paper route and tossed the rolled-up newspapers onto elegant porticos.

My mother came from one of the most illustrious families in New Orleans. Her mother was a Livaudais, and the Livaudais family had once owned the town, literally. Jacques Esnould de Livaudais, a corsair from Saint-Malo who made his living privateering for the East India Company, arrived in New Orleans in 1732. He was named captain of the port for his ability to navigate the dangerous passages of the Mississippi River, the shifting sands and mud bars, without wrecking, a critical skill that merchants rewarded him handsomely for. His descendants were the wealthiest landowners in the city; their plantation took up a good part of what is now the Garden District. If my mother had married a lawyer, she'd have been Mardi Gras Queen. Instead, she married a physical education teacher from Chicago. She might have resented our straightened circumstances but she never had a bad day while my father was alive.

❦

One of the first words I ever learned was "gym." My father coached at the exclusive Isidore Newman School, a prep academy that was just a few blocks away from our house. Each day my mother would drive me by the school grounds, and pretty soon I learned that's where my dad was. One afternoon when I was still a toddler I screamed out "Gym!" because I wanted to be with him. From then on, she dropped me off there every afternoon.

My father led a bunch of private school boys to three state titles and fifteen straight district championships, despite a rather carefree, nonchalant pose. He was the soul of generosity—which is what teaching is, after all, imparting to others. He was probably the best giver I ever knew, even though he had no money. He gave of himself, all the time, to his players, and the greatest gift he gave us was confidence and self-assurance.

I was one of those perpetually sweaty, dirt-grimed kids, always running, always keeping score at something. Each day when school was over, I played on the sidelines while my dad practiced his teams in Newman's old gym, which was a stifling, un-air-conditioned hot box. I was born a good athlete, with a weirdly versatile physical aptitude, and on top of that I was a worker. I shot thousands of baskets when I was a kid and soon enough became a dead-eyed shooter and passer on the basketball court. I was also one of the best young pitchers in town.

In the early evening, I would shower in the Newman locker room, and then, hair slick, I would walk back home holding my father's hand through the New Orleans twilight, past the broad porches of old mansions, their white trim glowing in the dark. Some of the houses were more cared for than others; the neglected ones peeled and sagged, like old ladies who misapplied their makeup. We'd stroll past shabby old oaks and palmettos, inhaling the night-blooming jasmine. Neighbors would wave and call out a lazy "Heey."

My father rarely treated anything seriously, especially games. He wasn't one of those grim, domineering Little League dads to whom games were the ultimate character tests. They were amusements. Play to him was just that: play. "If it's not fun, it ain't worth it," he'd say.

Here's all you need to know about Skeets Tuohy. On the wall of his locker room he put a picture of himself, blown up to eight feet tall, holding a Dixie beer can in one hand and a whistle in the other. A slogan read, "I Am Skeets Tuohy, Do As I Say, Not As I Do!" It was the last thing you saw coming out of the locker room. You think his players didn't hit the court loose and laughing?

My baseball games were social occasions for him. He'd stop at the concession where they sold beer and gaze at the field with one eye, but mostly he'd sit and laugh with his pals who wanted to buy him a cold one. Even the coaches he would regularly beat wanted to drink with him. He never paid for a beer—and he never went thirsty. When the ballpark lights would go off, he'd still be there, telling stories late into the night.

But beneath his relaxed veneer and apparent casualness, my father had a quiet intensity. At bottom he was a tough Chicago Irishman. At Newman he shaped a procession of short, slow, affluent white boys into a flamboyant, high-scoring dynasty. One of the ways he did so was with a combativeness drill:

He would place a basketball at half-court and then divide us into two squads and send us under each basket. With the blow of his whistle, a boy from each side of the gym would sprint to half-court and try to take possession of the ball—and there were no rules about what you could do to each other. You could kill the other guy, if that's what it took.

We were the crown jewel of the school and we elicited rage and envy from our rivals. Newman was an unlikely sports mecca. It was established in 1903 as a trade school for Jewish orphans by Isidore Newman, a local philanthropist who had founded the Maison Blanche department store chain. By the time I was a boy it had grown into an elite academy of handsome brick and gray stone on eleven lush acres. The student body was still predominantly Jewish, but now they were the children of the wealthy. To give you an idea, the yearly tuition now is about twenty thousand dollars. Some of Newman's famous alums include former *Time* magazine editor Walter Isaacson (whose uncle was the team doctor and who once put a lot of stitches in me while chewing a cigar) and the Manning boys, Peyton and Eli.

My father turned Newman's gym into one of the most popular, roar-filled sports arenas in the city. His teams would run up the score—and then run right off the floor without even shaking hands. Kids from all over town coveted a Newman jersey, and crowds jammed our bleachers past fire-code capacity. But our opponents hated us.

My mom was a model sports mother and coach's wife. The Tuohy kids never missed a practice no matter how many parts of the city she had to drive to. She was a one-woman cheering squad and, trust me, the other side was outnumbered. I can still remember my elegant-mannered mother sitting in the stands as the livid fans from other schools booed my father. She would sit up and yell back at them in her soft-as-a-fern southern accent, "You are UGLY people! You were uuuuugly last year and you are uuuugly this year!"

We wore sharp green uniforms, which my father insisted on buying new every year. The Newman administration would complain about spending all that money every season, but my father knew something about the pride of a garment and its effect on young wearers.

"Listen, the way I look at it, it takes fifteen years to become a good basketball player but it only takes fifteen minutes to look like one," he said. "And, by God, we're going to look like players every day. If we do nothing else, we're going to look like players."

Pride was very important to us—it was the fuel we played on, especially given that we didn't always have the advantage of size or the most talent. Another sign my father hung in the Newman locker room read, "Poise Plus Pressure Plus Pride Equals Success."

When other, more ordinary teams huddled up, they would chant a perfunctory "One-two-three-together!" But we were different—we were prouder. As we stood in our tight circle we would bark out in unison, with manly voices deep from our chests as if we were full-grown marines:

"A-HUNDRED-PERCENT-In-Every-Way-PRIDE!!!"

We were proud of everything—of our uniforms, of our coach, of our fluid, attacking style of play. We were known as the Greenies, for our school colors, and my father gave us our own flashy green and white basketballs to warm up with. We were the height of suave as we executed my father's run-and-gun philosophy. He had yet another saying and it was posted up on the wall, next to that poster of him.

It said, "Shoot to Get Hot. Shoot to Stay Hot."

We ran slick offensive sets and we switched defenses fifty times a game to confuse the other team. We poured it on shamelessly. It wasn't unusual for us to put ninety points on the board and if there had been a three-point line in those days, we'd have tried to score a thousand.

I never remember taking a shot and looking at the bench, afraid of a reprimand. My father wanted us to play freely, and we did. While other kids were afraid of pressure, we laughed at it. Pressure was something to be met head-on and relished, a contest within the contest.

"Just shoot," he'd say.

When I hesitated he'd say, "Son, what's the matter? Just shoot."

Once, I stepped to the free throw stripe with a game on the line and the gym falling into a tense silence. From across the court I could hear my father yell in a mocking tone, "If you miss these free throws . . . you're not eating supper tonight!"

✤

Thanks to my father, I had absolutely no conscience or hesitation with the basketball in my hands. When I was a freshman in high school, we made it to the state semifinals and, as time wound down, we found ourselves trailing by two points. With just a couple of seconds left, my father called time-out, turned to the bench, and gestured me into the game. I was the skinniest, youngest kid on either team. I had grown six inches that year, and stood six foot one, yet I weighed only 127 pounds. There was consternation in the stands as I ran on the floor. There was even more consternation when one of my teammates in-bounded the ball by passing it straight to me. What was Coach Tuohy doing, the fans murmured, giving the ball to his own kid, whose arms were thinner than sapling branches? But my father knew what kind of monster he had created.

I took a couple of swift dribbles—and launched a shot from just past half-court. It was a forty-footer . . . and it sailed through the net at the buzzer, to send the game into overtime, amid bedlam.

That exemplified what kind of leader he was and the kinds of players he taught us to be. He simply had no use for people who took pressure too seriously. Nor did he have any use for adults who pushed kids too hard and ruined their innate love of games. In fact, he had a policy for dealing with overinvolved parents.

"Sure, you can come talk to me about your kid," he'd say. "But for every minute you talk to me, that's a minute he's not going to get to play."

He had very few rules: you showed up, you behaved, and if you went to school, that was fine, too. He took an unusual approach to practices. We practiced for an hour and twenty minutes—full out—and then it was over. His philosophy was that we should *want* to be at practice. "You should never see the best athletes in school walking the halls at three thirty," he'd say. Which meant, if kids didn't want to come out for his team, he had created the wrong environment. He believed that we needed an outlet and he was merely there to provide the facility for it.

He taught us the proper fundamentals—"Elbows in, spread your palms, follow through"—and the right principles. His message was simple: behind any kind of confidence is conditioning and behind any inspiration is hard work. "You want credit, get a MasterCard," he'd say.

We played all the time, year-round, and outworked everybody. In the summers we rode our bikes all over town, looking for pickup games. We cruised through the poorer districts, where street musicians lamented on street corners—"*Do you know what it means to miss New Orleans, I miss it both night and day.*" We sought out players who were bigger and better than we were, so we could improve. Every night from seven to nine the Newman gym was open and all the best talent in New Orleans would come out to play.

My father wanted us to master the fundamentals until they became second nature and to play the game so fast that there wasn't much time to think. If a kid had to think, it was usually too late. Once, a great player of ours named Paul Inman started to explain himself to my father by saying, "Well, Coach, I think—"

Dad stopped him right there. "Have I ever once asked you to think?" he said. "Why would you start now?"

We were smart alecks and we got that quality straight from Skeets Tuohy, too. Every year Newman paid for my father to go to the national high school coaches' convention. One day in a faculty meeting a science teacher questioned the expense and complained that sports was overemphasized. Why didn't Newman bother sending him to a convention for science teachers? he wanted to know.

Dad leaned forward and said, "What was your record last year?"

❦

But underneath my father's laughing nature, he was under more strain than anyone realized. Maybe it was the combination of drinking and stress. Or perhaps he felt more tension in all of those high-scoring games and district championships than we knew. Or maybe he just inherited a time bomb in his genes. The cause was irrelevant—what mattered to me was the result. During the spring of my freshman year, my energetic, high-spirited father—at the age of just forty-one—was at

Galatoire's having lunch with friends when he suffered a massive stroke. He dropped to the floor, speechless and immobilized. High blood pressure had caused a blood clot in his brain.

He was rushed to the hospital to undergo brain surgery to remove the clot. During the hours-long operation he died on the operating table and had to be resuscitated. Although he survived, in the days and weeks after he regained consciousness it became apparent he was 90 percent incapacitated. He couldn't speak and he was completely paralyzed on the right side of his body.

He spent months in the hospital. When he was finally released, he was wheelchair bound and faced years of rehabilitation. Our house had seven short steps leading to the front door—yet he was incapable of climbing them. Even if he had been able to get inside, the cottage was simply too small for him to maneuver in his wheelchair. It was an impossible situation.

My parents had little choice but to move in with my grandparents, whose home was larger and had a flat entrance. They took with them my younger brother, Seamus, who was just eleven at the time. Meanwhile, my older sister, Sarah, went off to Louisiana State University, which was devastating for me because she had always been there for me, whether using her last store discount to buy me my only suit, or letting me drive her car, or just giving me the moral support every teen needs. My older brother, Edward, and I were left alone in the house. He was seventeen, about to be a senior at Newman, and I was fifteen.

My grandparents' house wasn't far away, on the edge of the Garden District, and it was easy enough to get there. But my father needed almost constant care and my mother was overwhelmed. With a disabled husband came enormous financial and emotional burdens. She had to go to work to help support us and found jobs with a local Catholic newspaper and a drugstore.

I went to see my father as often as I could. The sight of him in a wheelchair, his body half ruined and his ambition stunted, should have been emotionally devastating. But it wasn't. It quickly became obvious to me that he had not lost his remarkable buoyancy. Though he couldn't talk much, he could still laugh—and he laughed all the time. He could also cuss, because it came natural. The first word he learned to say after he came to was: "S——." It was a reflexive nonthought, and he'd use it, a lot. To me, it sounded beautiful.

My father never really worked again. After years of physical therapy he was finally able to get out of his wheelchair, but he did not recover the use of his right side. He gradually learned to walk again, leaning on a cane and dragging his foot. He also learned to speak again, after a fashion. Most people could barely understand him—but I could understand him just fine. Yet he never complained, and my impression was that he would have lived perfectly happily this way, every day, for the rest of his life. As it was, he would only survive a few more years.

❦

Our family had very little before my father's stroke, but now there was even less. I felt completely overmatched economically. I was forever looking up. It seemed that everyone I knew stood on a higher rung than I did—my schoolmates, my teammates, and my neighbors. They had their parents at home, they lived in grander houses, they had better and newer clothing, and they had lunch money in their pockets.

But I also discovered that some people in the world were willing to reach down, grab me, and pull me up. I will never forget how good that felt. My father had always been an open-hearted guy, but now people were openhearted with *us*, and I saw how much it meant. We were sustained by generosity. My father's coaching colleagues went to the local NBA team, the New Orleans Jazz, and organized a fund-raising day in his honor, donating the entire proceeds of a game to our family. My mother's brothers Bodie, Jacques, and Peter Michell were endlessly good to us, as were Jacques's wife, Wendy, and Bodie's wife, Danielle, my godmother. Then there were the kind-hearted souls at Newman, who granted all of the Tuohy kids free tuition for the rest of their high school years, even though our father no longer worked there. People did so many things for me that weren't a big deal—to them. Ever since, I've known how little it really takes to give someone a big leg up.

One of my teammates and closest friends in the world was a guy named Max Hart. We were complete opposites: he was Jewish, I was Catholic; he was affluent, I was not. His dad was an eye doctor, while mine was a gym teacher. He was a year older than me but he had four sisters at home, and he let me hang around to even up the numbers. He adopted me as a younger brother of sorts.

Max always seemed to recognize what I needed. For instance, I was the only kid on the team without a car. Max never mentioned it. Instead, he would just stay at the gym until I'd finished showering and then give me a ride wherever I needed to go. Five nights a week, I'd come out of the locker room to find him sitting there, waiting for me, jingling his car keys in his hand.

I never had to ask for his help, which was the thing I was most grateful for. He gave me his friendship and his support with a happy heart. Years later I would recognize that quality for what it was: Max was a cheerful giver. Helping me out wasn't a burden to him at all.

There were days when I had no lunch money in my pocket. I didn't know where a meal was going to come from, and I had a healthy appetite because I was constantly on the baseball field or a basketball court. I got pretty creative about finagling ways to feed myself. I'd go in the gym at noon and try to bait someone into making a bet with me: if I made fifty free throws in a row without missing, they'd have to buy my lunch. Or I would sneak into a movie theater with my friends and, when the popcorn stand attendant turned his back, I'd filch a bucket of popcorn.

Max sensed when I was hungry—which was often—and he would always buy me a burger. He'd say he needed to eat something and he'd take me along with him. Then he'd quietly pay for both of us, without comment. Again, I wouldn't have to ask. Which was a huge relief to me because, as much as I liked a burger and as hungry as I was for one, I never would have opened my mouth. I had too much pride. Asking would have made me a little less than who I wanted to be. I would rather stay quiet and ignore my growling stomach.

The experience of going without shaped me. It made me determined, for the rest of my life, to be as good as Max about anticipating the needs of others. To this day I feel lousy if someone has to ask for help, because I know the difference it can make in how you feel about yourself.

Other kids and their families helped me, too. My friend Paul Sterbcow loaned me a quarter at least three days a week. I always seemed to be a quarter short of soothing my hunger: I'd have one dollar in my pocket, but a burger and fries at the school cafeteria would cost a buck and a quarter. One more twenty-five-cent piece and I could get full. I'd say, "Hey, Paul, lend me a quarter?" He always gave it.

When the school day ended, Newman families were always having me over for dinner. My classmates' mothers loved to feed me. By my sophomore year I still only weighed about 130 pounds and all of those bighearted Jewish mothers assumed I didn't have enough to eat. I was completely healthy, but they worried about me.

Paul Sterbcow would say, "You have to come to dinner at our house, because my mother saw you the other day and says you aren't getting enough food. She thinks you're like one of those African kids in *National Geographic* who hasn't eaten." So I'd go to the Sterbcows' and they'd pound the food into me—they just kept bringing it.

I will forever be grateful to the Jewish mothers of Isidore Newman, because by the time I was a senior I weighed 145 pounds and felt really good about myself.

❦

Despite the loss of my father, my athletic career continued to flourish, thanks to a giving man named Billy Fitzgerald. A couple of years before his illness my father had had the good eye and sense to hire Billy, a former minor league ballplayer, to coach Newman's junior varsity teams. Billy was a cussing, demanding, hard-charging guy, and initially I feared him. I was in seventh grade the first time I ever watched him drill a team and I still remember turning to my friends and saying, "Oh, God, please don't let me get to eighth grade."

After my father had his stroke, Billy became the varsity coach. I probably should have resented him because he took over my dad's job, but somehow I didn't. Maybe it was because Billy never tried to replace Skeets Tuohy. Newman named Billy "acting head coach" and, even when it became apparent that my father would never return to work, Billy refused to make the title permanent and insisted on calling himself the "acting head coach" for the next several years in honor of my father. It was another example of cheerful giving, a simple, sensitive gesture he made out of respect for my dad. I don't know if anyone else noticed it—but I did. I've never forgotten it.

I played my heart out for him. Billy's style was completely different from my father's, but his impact on us—and on later generations of Newman athletes that included Peyton Manning—proved to be just as uplifting. We revered him for making men out of us, so much so that more than thirty years later my classmate and friend Michael Lewis wrote a book about the life-altering experience of playing for him entitled *Coach*.

Looking back on those years now, I realize that Billy was then hardly more than a kid himself, and he must have been under considerable pressure. He was just twenty-eight when he inherited the No. 1 high school basketball job in the city from a local legend and he had four small kids of his own at home. But to us he was never anything but a towering and even heroic figure of authority.

We had a funny relationship. We had conflicts all the time but they never seemed to matter. Billy would scream and holler at me, but I really didn't mind—other people screamed and hollered at me, too. From him, I liked it.

Billy ran us half to death. We were always sprinting through suicide drills or doing ladder calisthenics up and down the court. He was uncompromising, too: he kicked my brother Ed off the baseball team when he caught him smoking after a game.

Billy could use very good, uh, French. We had a lot of flair on the court and sometimes when we admired ourselves too much, he'd get furious at us. If he thought we were loafing, or were right on the edge of being too cute, he'd say, "Quit f—— around!" He said it a lot. Once, he lost his temper and threw a ball in practice and it accidentally hit a kid in the head. I was a smart aleck, so I said, "Quit f—— around!" He whirled and just tore me up.

But mostly we did everything he asked of us. We won back-to-back state titles in my junior and senior years, and it got to the point where his ethic was ours. We had a great player named Fain Hackney, whose father, Sheldon, was a noted historian and the president of Tulane University. One day Hackney appeared for practice with a ponytail. We wouldn't let him play. Billy didn't even have to tell us. We just said, "Nope, you're not going to play like that. Get it cut." And he did.

The greatest favor Billy Fitzgerald did for me was to preserve my love of the game—which was important, because it was all I had. After my father's stroke, I could have soured on basketball. Billy could have mishandled the bereaved boy I was or made it awkward for his former boss's son. But playing for Billy those years, I became everything I was supposed to be. I hit thirty-seven points in the state championship game, playing with a cheerful arrogance that said, "I have the ball and you don't. You can have it when I'm finished with it." It was the high point of my high school years—and I'm glad I have that glowing memory, because it was the last time I would play basketball without regret or anxiety, the last time the game would just be a game.

I had a choice to make. I was a good enough baseball player that the Cincinnati Reds were scouting me. I got a call from the organization, telling me they intended to draft me. I thought about it and said, "Don't." While the quick money was tempting, playing professional baseball didn't interest me all that much, mainly because I knew I had to have a college degree if I was going to make anything of myself. A scholarship was my one chance to get an education; it wasn't like I could afford to pay my own way. And if I blew this chance to go to college, I'd never have another. On draft day, the Reds called again. They still wanted to take me. I repeated, "Don't." I was going to finish my education.

I had scholarship offers to play college basketball, though my choices were limited. Tulane and Louisiana State were just down the road; unfortunately, they didn't recruit me. My teachers at Newman wanted me to go to the Ivy League, but I preferred a school with a band and a real fight song—that's how serious my college search was. Ole Miss was popular, and pretty, and just a two-hour drive away, and they offered me a full ride. My father said, "You could go to some places and be just another good player, but they haven't had many good ones at Ole Miss. You go there, you'll make a difference." He was right. The way I recall it, I was better than average at Ole Miss—but their memory of me is that I was great. (There isn't any video to tell the tale, so I'm happy to let their estimation of my legacy stand.)

I felt very fortunate to be offered a basketball scholarship to Ole Miss. But you know what the best thing about it was? The unlimited food. Suddenly, eating was no longer a concern. Getting that scholarship—that was a good day.

⚜

A coach can give a lot to a kid, but he can take a lot from him, too. He can strip him of his dignity, break down his body, and ruin his pleasure in the game. At Ole Miss, I learned that sad lesson the hard way. Thanks to one man, playing basketball turned into a grinding chore, something to be endured while I got a degree.

The head coach at Ole Miss was Bob Weltlich, a martinet who earned every bit of his nickname, "Kaiser Bob." His teaching staples were physical overwork and verbal abuse. He was a coarse, big-voiced man who had learned his methods as a longtime assistant to Bobby Knight, first at Army and then at Indiana, where in 1976 he was on the staff of the Hoosiers when they went 32-0 to win the national championship. He knew something about basketball but had no discernible compassion for his players. Nor did he appear to tolerate the idiosyncrasies of talent. He would say things like, "Titles are won with good character—not characters."

Ole Miss was his first job as head coach and he took every opportunity to show us who was boss. In my first practice as a freshman, he conducted a bone-crushing full-contact drill. As the practice wore on, I wondered if he *wanted* someone to get hurt. And they did. A player named Scotty Field took a brutal fall, came down wrong, and shattered his elbow. While Scotty lay there screaming, with his arm bent wrong, I tried not to throw up.

Weltlich just said, "Let's go, other end." He gestured us to the opposite half of the court to continue practice, while the medical people attended to Scotty.

That set the pattern for my four years playing under Weltlich. We never finished a season with more than ten players. We'd start with fifteen and by the end of the season we'd be down to eight or nine. The rest would all be banged up.

I was the team's point guard, and Weltlich seemed to go out of his way to torment me. He believed in a walk-it-up-the-court style and he was apparently so intent on forcing me to accept his system that he never called me by name—not once in four years. He just called me by number.

"Hey, twelve!" he'd shout.

My lowest point during my first season was a road trip to Illinois for a tournament at Christmastime. We got beat in the finals by Illinois State, a nationally ranked team, on Christmas Eve, and then spent the rest of the night traveling. We rode a bus for four hours, followed by a commerical flight to Memphis, and then took another two-hour bus ride to campus. Weltlich never said a word to us the whole trip. When we finally pulled into Oxford in the dreary early hours of Christmas morning, I was exhausted and limping, because I had torn some cartilage in my right knee. As we trooped off the bus, Weltlich announced that we were to be dressed and ready "in thirty minutes" for films and practice.

We trudged into the film room and sat there like hostages. If he had used duct tape, he couldn't have made me feel more like a prisoner. Then, as the film projector started up, Weltlich leaned over my chair and spoke into my ear.

"Hey, twelve," he said. "Merry f—— Christmas."

We practiced three times that day. Nobody could go to church. Nobody could eat lunch with their families.

By the end of the season we were in open rebellion. Two players wrote up a petition asking for his removal, and every single one us of signed it. But when we presented it to administration officials, it backfired. The administration refused to discipline Weltlich and we were hung out to dry.

In 1980 we earned an invitation to the NIT tournament and beat Grambling in the first round, a huge deal because never in its entire history had Ole Miss appeared in a postseason basketball game. But we had a tough draw: in the next round we had to play on the road against a very good Minnesota team that starred future NBA Hall of Famer Kevin McHale. When we lost, Weltlich went into a rage.

That was the final game for senior John Stroud, who was probably the greatest player in Ole Miss basketball history. He was also our floor leader, as well as my roommate on the road. But instead of consoling Stroud, or thanking him for what he had given the team, this is what Weltlich did.

He gathered up all of Stroud's clothes and threw them into a urinal.

"You played like s——," he said, "so I'm treating you like s——."

Weltlich made Stroud collect the garments out of the stinking urinal, dress in them, and wear them home.

I'd never been a quitter but by now I wanted off of that team. But I was trapped because I needed the grant money. I was worried that Weltlich would take away my scholarship or bench me, and he knew it. July 6 was the annual renewal date of our scholarships, and each year as the date came around we felt especially insecure about our futures. I remember when he turned to one kid and said, "You can't play here. See me Monday and give me three schools, and I will help you transfer." That was what life was like playing for the guy.

Somehow, I performed decently under him but, for the first time in my life, I played mechanically. It was a job, a means to an end. I set an NCAA record for assists, and two of my marks still stand in the Southeastern Conference—for career assists (830) and single season assists (260)—but that was mainly because Weltlich practically threatened to drown me in the toilet if I shot the ball instead of passed it. And since he had thrown Stroud's clothes in the urinal, I had no doubt that my clothes were in play.

By Christmas of my third season, I'd finally had enough. I marched into his office.

"I'm going home," I said.

"Sit down," he said.

"Nope. I'm standing up."

I was ready to fight him. I wasn't going to put up with his abuse for one more minute and he could see it in my face.

"You think you're gonna keep crapping on me," I told him, "but it's not gonna happen anymore. I'm done."

Weltlich stayed calm and by the end of the conversation he talked me out of leaving, mainly by reminding me that I couldn't afford to quit.

After that confrontation, he eased up a little bit, or at least left me alone. I became team captain and made All-SEC, and in the spring of that year we won the Southeastern Conference tournament title, still the only championship in Ole Miss basketball history.

But the damage was done. Weltlich had not taught me anything, or given me anything. He had only taken something away: my pleasure in basketball. I began thinking more about finding a career after school, and for the first time I really hit the books. I wasn't a strong student—as I like to say, I made the top half of the class possible—but in my final year at Ole Miss I made decent grades and was named to the All-SEC Academic Team.

Weltlich never congratulated me for anything. It was traditional for most universities to hold a senior day to honor their graduating players. Before a game the players would be introduced and receive some individual recognition, maybe a round of applause and some flowers. Weltlich didn't even do this much for us. As he put it to me one day, "I'd have a senior day but I'd be afraid they'd boo you."

Shortly after I graduated, Weltlich went on to become head coach at the University of Texas, where his methods were just as tough. But his players at UT were less acquiescent. In 1983, his first season, a dozen Longhorns quit or were thrown off the team and he had to recruit a male cheerleader to make up a full roster. You know what his poor treatment of players got him? A career record of 300-335 and a whole lot of angry kids.

In 2001, our Southeastern Conference championship team held a twenty-year reunion, and almost everyone came back for it. Weltlich showed up, too. When he stood up to speak, he actually tried to apologize for the way he treated us. But four or five players shouted him down. "We don't want to hear it!" somebody yelled from the back of the room. "It's too late!" someone else hollered. That's how strongly we felt about what he'd done to us. That's how much he had taken from us.

☙

Three things relieved my misery at Ole Miss and made my four years there a more positive experience: my fabulous teammates, my first car, and meeting Leigh Anne.

The car came from my older sister, Sarah, who loaned me her junker, a beat-up old Chevy Vega, and I loved her for it. A subcompact two-door with a hatchback, it had no air-conditioning and the horsepower of a broken-down mule. There were two slight hills on the way to Vaught Hall, the athletic dorm, and I couldn't make it up the second one. I had to drive the long way around and take the flat approach to the dorm.

But I loved that car. I was so proud of having my own wheels that I was always offering the team rides to and from practice. I'd pull into the parking lot at Vaught Hall with a bunch of six-foot-four black guys crammed in the hatchback. To me, that car was a beautiful thing.

As for Leigh Anne, she was hard to avoid. In fact, she literally threw herself at me.

We were sophomores the first time we came face-to-face. In December 1979, Ole Miss won a big basketball game over nationally ranked Alabama, and I hit the game-winning free throw with only a second left on the clock. Afterward, the campus was practically writhing in celebration and the revelry was especially intense at the Kappa Alpha House, which was hosting a boxer-shorts-and-sunglasses theme party. That's what everybody had to wear. (Or, more accurately, it's what everybody *else* had to wear—I don't do dress-up.) The place was swarming with undergrads in all kinds of goofy get-ups. There were coeds in dark Ray-Bans and flannel briefs and frat guys in wraparound shades and cotton shorts with polka dots on them.

I stepped through the fraternity's front door into a roaring, liquor-soaked, underwear-clad mob. The minute I crossed the threshold, I saw a girl coming at me like a blaze. She had waist-long blond hair with four colors of sunshine in it. She was wearing Mickey Mouse sunglasses and boxers. She jumped into my arms and kissed me. The kiss held for a second and then she was gone. She disappeared into the boisterous, damp crowd like a flash.

I stood there dumbfounded. Standing next to me was my girlfriend's sister, in town to see the game. Understandably, she was looking at me somewhat suspiciously. I turned to her and said with as much earnestness as I could muster, "I swear to God I have no idea who that was."

True—but what I didn't say was that I had every intention

of finding out. Who wouldn't want to date that? It was the best welcome I'd ever had.

We moved deeper into the crowd, and as soon as I caught sight of the blond girl again, I turned to one of my buddies and asked, "Who *is* that?" The answer came back that she was Leigh Anne Roberts, a varsity cheerleader and a prominent member of the Kappa Delta sorority house. Though she was only a sophomore, she was one of the prettiest and most sought after coeds on campus. And she was already known as a go-getter who was so organized and overscheduled with sorority campaigns that she kept an agenda planner. In those days, nobody kept a planner in college.

At some point during that wild evening, Leigh Anne came over and properly introduced herself, and within a few weeks we were seeing each other. We didn't anticipate that our romance would become serious, because we were both dating other people—in her case, several people—but it did, pretty quickly. We fell into a routine. In the afternoons, I had basketball and she had cheerleading practice, and then we would get together and study until nine or ten. After that we'd go over to Shoney's and order something to eat, and many nights we'd sit there and talk until three or four a.m.

By temperament we were very different, but somehow our relationship worked. I was a beer-drinking Catholic; she was an abstemious Baptist. I was laid-back, drawling, easygoing. Leigh Anne was a pure type A. She didn't like failure and she had an iron will. *You'd better have the mustard to hang with her*, I thought to myself, *or she'll absolutely stomp on you.* When she wanted to get something done, she didn't much care who was in her way. She was either going to solve all the world's problems—or just take over the world.

Years later, our son Sean Junior would say about her, "Mom's really a soft touch deep down—somewhere."

People who were deceived by her cuteness were asking for trouble. She reminded me of the Killer Rabbit of Caerbannog, that bunny in the Monty Python movie. The rabbit looked all sweet and unmenacing on the outside—just a cute, fluffy bunny. But if you tried to pass, all of a sudden it bared its teeth and grabbed you by the neck. As Tim says to Sir Galahad: "Look, that rabbit's got a vicious streak a mile wide! It's a killer!"

That was Leigh Anne.

Everybody, including me, was a little afraid of her. Leigh Anne eliminated the gray areas in life; if something was wrong, by God, it was wrong. But here was the most important thing about her: *she* didn't have to be right; she just wanted *it* to be right. Once you understood that about her, you didn't just love her, you respected her.

I learned about her absolute insistence on getting it right when she took on Bob Weltlich—and backed him down. Leigh Anne didn't have much use for Weltlich in the first place because of the way he tormented me. But then I made the mistake of telling her about how he'd made a vulgar reference to her one day in practice when he was berating me. "You're getting too much p——," he had sneered at me.

Now, Leigh Anne did not cuss back then and still rarely does. Our friend Liz Marable claims she was in her mid-thirties before she heard Leigh Anne use profanity for the first time. Our daughter, Collins, was a little girl competing in a gymnastics meet, and the judges didn't give her the score Leigh

Anne felt she deserved. Leigh Anne muttered, "S——." Liz turned pale with shock and was crushed.

"It was like the Lord had come down and cussed," Liz said later.

So Leigh Anne was furious with Weltlich about his language—but she was even angrier about his implication. As a college student, Leigh Anne loved a good party but she was also very chaste. Her reputation was important to her and she took great care of it.

After cheerleading practice one day, she stalked up to Weltlich and fixed him with a death-ray glare. "Don't you *ever* use that word in reference to me again," she said. "You do and it'll be the last time you ever say it."

Weltlich looked sheepish and tried to apologize—maybe because he knew Leigh Anne's father was a U.S. marshal who packed a Magnum under his suit coat.

Another time, Leigh Anne went to Weltlich to complain about the sneakers the cheerleaders had to wear. They were flimsy and cheap compared to what the athletes got, and she wanted better ones. So she went into his office, carrying a pair contemptuously by their shoestrings like they were rat tails, and she dropped them right on his desk. "We want nicer shoes than this," she said. She got them, too.

I was sure she was going to get me benched or kicked off the team. I had just worked my way into some playing time and now I figured my career was over.

"I'm not that good," I told her. "It's not like I have leverage."

Nearly thirty years later, Leigh Anne is still behaving like that killer rabbit and she's still talking to people the same way. Me, I'm still trying to figure out whether to admire her style or wince at it. Sometimes I don't like it—I wish she'd relax and not yell at the coach and I'd prefer that she quit telling everybody in the stands who the idiots are. It's not like she's wrong. But as I say to her, "Sweetheart, we don't always have to be the ones who tell them."

               ❦

There are times when Leigh Anne's forthrightness comes in handy, though. For instance, she told *me* we were getting married. It was early in our senior year, and I was driving her to class one morning when she said, "Okay, it's time to get engaged." Then she reached into her pocket and pulled out a little box.

"Here's the ring," she said.

She had actually picked out the engagement ring she wanted and bought it.

"I've also chosen the date," she said. "June twelfth."

She had chosen twelve because it was my uniform number.

"Certainly you can remember that," she said.

I just nodded at her, openmouthed.

"Okay, I have to go to class now," she said.

She hopped out of the car, and I just sat there for a minute, absorbing what had just transpired. "I guess I'm getting married," I said to myself, and drove off.

By that point, I already knew I wanted to marry Leigh Anne, but it would have taken a lot longer for me to declare my intentions. As usual, she was a few steps ahead of me. That's the way it's always been between us and somehow it works. I guess you could say that where she's concerned, I'm very coachable.

When friends ask me how I've managed to forge such a happy marriage for twenty-eight years, I joke that it's because I don't have a huge need to be in charge. But the real answer is more difficult to articulate. How do you explain harmony? For whatever reason, we have it, even though we're very different. I'm a slow talker and more roundabout; she's quick-firing, easy to rile, and very assertive. My way of doing things takes three weeks; hers takes three minutes. We're both achievers—we just go about it differently. So who is right? I don't think either of us cares, which is probably one reason we don't have many arguments. What matters most is that we complement each other. And, on the important things, we understand each other almost perfectly.

Over the years, our differences have tended to be sources of interest, not conflict. She loves to do things for people they won't do for themselves—for one thing, she makes my clothes match. And she pushes people, opens new possibilities to them. For instance, I started going to church with her. When people ask me how I became an Evangelical, I say, "I married a girl way above my head." Which is true. I wanted to go to church and I wanted to go with her. So I went with her—and I liked it. I liked it a whole lot. If she were Jewish, I'd probably be Jewish right now.

Leigh Anne loves to show people things they've never seen before. Like the ocean. Taking a child to see the sea for the first time is one of her favorite things to do. "You've never seen the ocean before?" she exclaims, and the next thing you know, we're all going to Florida. We've done a lot of things we would never have done if not for Leigh Anne.

Our wedding was an exuberant affair at Central Church

in Memphis, a five-thousand-seat Evangelical pulpit. We should have charged admission. Fourteen of Leigh Anne's sorority sisters and fellow cheerleaders were the maids of honor and they claimed they deserved overtime pay because they put so much work into the flowers and the food. My friends from New Orleans interpreted the wedding as an excuse to drink and they set up a bar *inside* the church. My ballplayer teammates were all in the wedding and towered over the guests. The ceremony disconcerted our parents on both sides of the aisle. To make my mother happy, Leigh Anne allowed a Catholic priest to copreside with her Evangelical pastor, Jimmy Latimer. My mother still wasn't sure it was a real marriage. She swore I danced with snakes.

After we graduated and got married, our futures were vague. The New Jersey Nets drafted me, but as a six-foot-one white boy I didn't have the size or the talent to be a success in the NBA. Besides, my passion for the game was gone, so I declined to sign with them. I considered a high school coaching job, but the pay wasn't good enough. I had also been accepted to law school, but the idea of more years of study didn't appeal to me either.

I decided on a career in business. I was driven to make money—that's why I didn't become a coach like my father, which was probably my real calling. It's terrible to say, but it's the truth: I wanted to make a lot of money as quickly as possible. And I accomplished that soon enough. But once I started making money, I immediately developed the urge to give some of it to kids who didn't have any. Probably because I'd been such a grateful recipient as a boy, I tried to find ways to give money to kids who had less, kids who reminded me of myself. Gamers.

But, just as I was about to begin a career in business, I got an offer to play a summer of pro ball in a European league. Leigh Anne urged me to take advantage of it. As usual, she wanted me to experience something new. So with her generous blessing, I made the trip.

While I was in Europe playing basketball, my father was diagnosed with lung cancer. When I returned to Memphis after my summer tour, Leigh Anne met me at the airport. My wife of just three months had to tell me, "You've got to get back on a plane and fly to New Orleans. Your father is dying."

He lasted just three weeks after I came home—and he passed away on the day that the Newman gym was renamed the Tuohy Gymnasium in his honor. My dad was only forty-nine when he died. But, somehow, he'd made me feel as if I'd had him for a long time. I'd had the greatest dad in the world, and he'd been such an intensely loving father that I didn't feel cheated. Instead, I felt he was the one who was cheated.

Our first year of marriage was like two colliding waves, one of joy and one of sorrow. Because of what we'd been through together, Leigh Anne and I were perhaps more mature than some couples who get married just out of college, and I think we had a greater understanding of each other.

One important thing Leigh Anne and I had as we started our life together was a shared foundation of values. We were both hard workers and neither of us had grand pretensions. We both wanted to be successful but we also believed that true character was not measured by how much money we made or what social circles we mingled in. True character was about how we treated people. We would try to live by that principle and preach it to our children every day.

We also shared a theory: we were born to make a difference. It was up to us to put down some footprints in our community, to live for something more than just ourselves. If we could do that in any shape, form, or fashion, then it would be a blessing not just in someone else's life but in our own.

INTERLUDE

Tim McGraw

ACTOR

I THINK PEOPLE ENCOUNTER THESE KINDS OF CIRCUM-
stances all the time, but they don't confront them. *The Blind
Side* was about turning the car around and asking questions.
No one would have considered Sean and Leigh Anne bad
people for not stopping, no one would have thought worse of
them, no one would have even known.

It all just kind of fell together in the right place at the right
time with the right people and the right kid. It could have
been the wrong family that wanted to take somebody in and
the right kid, or it could have been the wrong kid and the right
family, and turned out disastrous.

It took a lot of heart and courage for this family to take
Michael in, but you also have to look at it through *his* eyes. It was
very scary and dangerous, how he was growing up, but imagine
being taken into this family and how different the lifestyle was?
For a kid from the projects to be taken into this wealthy white
family and go to this private school, you know that had to be a
lot scarier for him in some ways than the place he'd come from.

I almost didn't sign on to the film, but I got caught up in the kid's attitude. I had already done a football movie, *Friday Night Lights*, and I didn't want to do another. But there was something infectious about Michael's story. It just became about heart, about his determination. A lot of people did nice things for him, but he's the one who knuckled down and did it. It would have been easy for him to say "I can't deal with this new world" and go back to what he knew.

It's been so cool to be involved in a movie that allows you to follow the ongoing story. The great thing for the audience is that they could go to the movie on Saturday night and get up on Sunday and watch the actual guy play out his rookie season in the NFL. And he was in the running for Rookie of the Year, too.

The script was in a stack I had to read on vacation. I didn't think I would be interested, but I read it and it stuck with me. I realized it really wasn't about football at all. The story was about integrity and character and class more than anything. Then I found out Sandra was going to do it, and John Lee Hancock was going to direct, and all the reasons to do it started adding up, and the reasons not to do it didn't make sense anymore. I just couldn't say no to it.

One of my reservations was that it was a tough role because Leigh Anne's character is such a dynamo and Sean's character is more laid-back. Sean has to be the steady anchor that the family tethers itself to. You have to put forth this silent, strong guy that holds the family together and not be overshadowed. The challenge of the role was to stay within the realm of what's called for with the character but still have a presence that's strong. The challenge was to not get lost.

Sean and I have a lot in common. We both grew up in Louisiana and we were both athletes. Also, we're both married to women who run the show at home. I certainly feel we both married way over our heads. He has that "I've got to do what my wife tells me" look too, so maybe the role wasn't that much of a stretch for me.

Sean is very relaxed, sort of like me. There's not a lot of high emotion, and the hardest thing to do is play a character that doesn't have a huge range to start with. But he personifies the quiet strength that this family has. So the challenge was to portray this guy who is the baseline for everything—without jumping up and down and waving a flag saying, "Here I am."

2

Giving

LEIGH ANNE

God gives you money because he wants to see how you handle it.

—LEIGH ANNE TUOHY

I'M GONNA BE REAL HONEST WITH YOU: PEOPLE ASK some stupid questions. You can tell the short school bus picked them up.

"Did you ever think Sandra Bullock would play you in a movie?"

Sometimes I want to reply, "Yes, I got up this morning and thought, 'Sandra Bullock's going to play me in a movie today.'"

Sandy did a good job, by the way, and if she hadn't, I'd have told her in a second. She took some artistic license of course; maybe I wouldn't have hung those particular drapes. But what does it matter? Besides, she has fabulous ta-tas, which elated me.

I'm all about getting things done. Lip service is pretty cheap.

Anybody can get up and talk, or memorize a few scriptures and sound devout. In the end, what really matters is how you walk and how you live each day. After spending some time with me and asking all sorts of questions, Sandy finally decided I wasn't a fake. She said, "This is real with you." I didn't know what she was talking about. I said, "I don't have extensions in my hair?"

My family says I have "Truth Tourette's syndrome." That's what these outbursts of mine are now called, Truth Tourette's. A pastor recently put it more gently. He told me, "When you feel the Lord telling you to say something, you just say it."

Collins says, "Yeah, but we're the ones who have to live with it."

Despite my verbal outbursts, I'm not one of those "Do as I say" people. My husband and kids would tell you that I'm more of the "Do as I do and follow me" type. They call me the General. As Sean says, "You've got faults, but one of them ain't organization." You can see that in our French eclectic living room: all the items on the tables, from my Limoges porcelain boxes to the family pictures, are perfectly aligned. Sean and the kids like to tease me by moving an object just a fraction when I'm not looking. They'll turn the corner of a coffee table book slightly off angle and then sit there, wagering silent bets on how long it will take me. I'll walk into the room and know something's not right. I'll circle the coffee table two or three times. Then I'll absently reach over and put the book back where it was, while they stifle giggles.

I confess that I'm one of those people who clean before the housekeeper arrives. I'm always wiping everything down with Windex and 409 spray, because I can't stand to see a fingerprint. Our house is filled with fumes of ammonia and other cleaning agents. The last time Sean Junior went down with a bug I scoured until everything smelled like bleach. The kids claimed, "We're all going to die because we've inhaled so much cleanser."

They tend to exaggerate about my cooking, too. It's not that I can't cook. I just won't. I don't like all the disorder, the stains, the splatters, the scraps and leftovers. When I do cook—I make a lovely Christmas brunch—I cover all the surfaces in the kitchen with Saran Wrap and tinfoil, so they're splatter proof. The stovetop, the counters and backsplashes—everything's got a protective layer of plastic or foil. That way, no mess. Makes cleanup a breeze.

Southern women tend to be strong natured. It's kind of a characteristic, or in my case maybe a characteristic flaw. I have a talent for difficult projects and the will to see them through to the end. If I hear of something that needs to be done, especially where a child is concerned, it resonates with me, and I'm real impatient until it's accomplished. I don't just throw money at it.

But if money needs to be thrown, I can do that, too. One of my closest friends, Liz Marable, is a math teacher at Frederick Douglass, a large public high school in Memphis. It's in one of the city's most historic yet blighted neighborhoods and it has a lot of needs. Liz is very active in fund-raising, but sometimes she can get pretty frustrated. On Sunday when she goes to church, this is how she prays:

"Dear Lord, please put it in Leigh Anne's heart to get us a football field and a track."

The iron in me, as well as my love of order, comes from my father, Stanley Charles Roberts, who was a Korean war veteran and a U.S. marshal. My softness around the edges and my eye for color—as well as my compulsive cleaning habits—come from my mother, Virginia Cummings Roberts, who is an interior designer. They were both very loving and open-handed givers, but they were poles apart in how they went about it. My father was a tough-love type, stern and curt. My mother is so kindhearted that Sean says, "You could shoot her in the head, and, if she survived, the next day she'd forgive you and give the bullet back."

In our house there was a distrust of false piety. It came from my maternal grandmother, Virginia Collins Cummings, who lived with us a good deal of the time when I was growing up and who we all adored. Everyone called her "Virgie," except for my father, who wouldn't call her anything but "Miss Cummings." He waited on her with a courtesy I still remember and he would do anything for her. "Would you like an ice tea, Miss Cummings?" he'd ask. She had an old-fashioned spirituality, right down to the organ-pounding hymns she preferred, such as "That Old Rugged Cross." Every night she sat in her rocking chair and had a devotional, reading her Bible, yet she never sermonized. She simply lived her life according to the gospel. To her, conduct was much more important than words.

As she liked to put it, "Don't talk about it, sister. Live it."

That became the informal motto for our entire family. My mother was as consistent in her devotionals as my grandmother. "The most important person in your life is God," she'd tell me. She was a great believer in tithing: she and my father gave 10 percent of everything they earned to the Parkway Village Baptist Church, no matter how lean times were.

"Things are not important, people are," she would tell me.

My father was a more laconic, outwardly hard guy. He didn't say a whole lot, but you'd see him be generous to people in his own way. Whenever we ate out, at the end of the meal he'd open his wallet and drop a big tip on the table.

"What are you doing?" I'd ask.

"It's their living," he'd say, quietly.

Cops don't make much money, and that's basically what my father was. Our circumstances were comfortable, but there were years when my parents had to stretch a dollar. They were supporting Virgie as well as two children—I was five when my younger brother Stanford was born—and a law officer's salary wasn't exactly six figures.

After they tithed 10 percent, there wasn't a lot to spare, but my father gave more anyway. I can remember my mother looking over his pay stub and saying, "Why did you have United Way take so much out of your paycheck?" He also frequently sent twenty dollars a month to starving kids overseas through one of those Save the Children–type organizations. He had vivid memories of what the Korean War had done to the local children there, and every month a picture would arrive of another child he was sponsoring.

❦

You would never mistake my father for a pushover, though. The army made him who he was. Originally from Dearborn, Michigan, his family moved to Jackson, Tennessee, and bought a janitorial company. But the prospect of taking over the family business didn't appeal to him, so at seventeen he stole his older brother's birth certificate and enlisted in the army. He was inducted into the First Infantry Division, the "Big Red One," under the name Private Wesley Roberts, and then shipped to Europe to serve in the Cold War. In 1951 he joined the Seventh Infantry Division and was sent to Korea, where he served for two years. He saw combat in some of that war's bitterest fighting. He came back a corporal covered in decorations, including two Purple Hearts.

My father didn't talk much about his service except to say how brutal it was and to hint that he'd killed men in close combat. In one engagement, he went into a foxhole with thirty men and only three came out alive. He said that when the bullets started flying, the wildest guys in the unit—who had cussed the most and cursed God—suddenly began chanting fervent prayers. "Man, they started asking for forgiveness real quick." Once, someone said to him almost flippantly, "There are no atheists in foxholes." My dad just looked grim and said, "You don't know how true that is."

My father did much of his fighting on the Yalu River on the North Korea–China border, where Douglas MacArthur launched a major offensive. The men of the Seventh Division fought in pitiless cold until their feet were so frostbitten that they had to use their weapons as crutches. We could see that my father experienced some pain walking, but we didn't know whether he'd been seriously injured at the Yalu River or elsewhere in Korea. We only knew that he had a row of campaign ribbons and medals, which were framed, and that there were more decorations stashed away in some old jewelry boxes. But we didn't learn how meritorious his service had been until after he died, when we found a pile of newspaper clippings that described his military career. That's how little he bragged.

My father was just twenty-one when he was honorably discharged from the service. He returned home to Tennessee and became a small-town cop, the youngest man ever to join the Jackson Police Department. On a corner of his beat in downtown Jackson was a family-owned jewelry store, and while doing his rounds he liked to stop in to say hello to the very attractive salesgirl. Pretty soon he began stopping by more often, and when it got cold outside he'd come in and stay awhile. After a few months of this, he and my mom got engaged.

In 1961, he was appointed a deputy U.S. marshal under President John F. Kennedy and assigned to the Memphis office. As a marshal he joined a tough and illustrious group that was proud of its five-point star badge and its history. Established in 1789, the service is the oldest form of law enforcement in the country and the strong arm of the Justice Department. Over the years its members have done everything from chasing the Dalton Gang across the Old West to busting up stills during Prohibition. Some of the men who had served as marshals included Bat Masterson, Wyatt Earp, and Wild Bill Hickok.

Stanley Roberts looked and acted every inch a lawman. He wore close-fitting white T-shirts under his dress shirt and kept his hair cut "high and tight." With a .357 Magnum strapped to his side, a long khaki trench coat draped over his shoulders, and a cigarette dangling, he looked like something out of *Dragnet*. He was a heavy smoker who favored Winston 100s, the gold pack. He was gruff and handsome and he exuded authority. Years later when Tommy Lee Jones starred as a marshal in the film *The Fugitive*, all of my friends called me and said, "Oh, my God, that was your dad when we were in high school."

He was very regimented—whenever he opened a jar, he dated it with a black marker, until everything in the pantry and in the freezer had labels in block letters. He applied the same orderliness and simplicity to everything. There were no moral gray areas. He very tersely told you what to do, with no beating around the bush. You always knew where you stood with my dad.

Any boy dating me knew he would be given a close inspection by my father. The doorbell would ring and within a minute or two my date would often be squirming under my father's stare. Sometimes my dad would reach into his wallet and pull out a ten-dollar bill.

"Here," he'd say, handing the boy the ten. "Go get your hair cut and you can come back for her next Friday night."

That must have happened half a dozen times in my life.

He was the ultimate authority back then, and you didn't disobey. His standard line was, "I'm gonna tell you once." Once you heard that, you did your best to stay on the right side of the line he'd drawn. For instance, he'd say, "It's real simple, sweetheart. If you don't speed, you won't get a speeding ticket. And if you don't drink, you can't get a DUI." When I got my license, I became a very careful driver.

His most unyielding rule was that I was never, ever to ride a motorcycle. As a cop he had seen a bunch of motorcycle wrecks, and there were always dead bodies on the scene. "I've never been to a motorcycle wreck where there was anyone left alive," he said.

Of all the rules to break, I chose that one, which led to the only butt whipping I ever got. When I was sixteen, I accepted a ride on the back of a friend's motorcycle. Someone saw me and mentioned it to him, and when he gave me the chance to tell the truth about it, I lied. He whipped his belt off and gave me about six good licks. He said, "Don't you *ever* ride on a motorcycle. I don't know what part of that wasn't clear to you. But I hope it's very clear to you now." It was.

My father had a foolproof way of making sure there were no misunderstandings. He carried his .357 every day, and at night when he came home he would unholster it and put it on his dresser, along with his badge and his money clip. It was a nightly ritual in our house to hear the clunk of those heavy, masculine items as he laid them down on the varnished wood.

As we got a little older, my dad began to worry that his children might find the gun intriguing. His dresser was a high-boy but it wasn't so tall that I couldn't figure out how to get up there if I wanted to. But since my dad didn't want to come home after a tough day and have to hide his gun, he decided to make us *very* aware of what that gun could do.

Not long after I turned twelve he took me out to Stanton, Tennessee, where Virgie had a house in the countryside. Then he called me into the backyard and produced a live rabbit. He walked a few paces from the rabbit, turned, and shot it. The explosion thundered across the landscape, and the bullet obliterated the rabbit, leaving nothing but a bloody headless pulp. "That is what this gun does," he said. "It's not a toy. You don't touch it. You don't play with it." It may sound like a cruel exercise, but my father preferred a dead rabbit to a dead child. It worked. Let me tell you, from then on I had a keen awareness of what that gun could do.

Later, when I was old enough, my father taught me how to use a firearm and insisted that I pack one in my purse. After *The Blind Side* came out, one newspaper article called me a "gun-toting Republican Christian." That was only partly accurate. I've voted for both Republican and Democratic candidates—in fact, I cross party lines all the time. But I do carry a gun wherever I go. Whenever somebody asks me what sort of gun, I tell the truth.

I say, "I have a bunch of them."

❦

In high school I was always the good girl. I was so respectful of my dad that I never wanted to disappoint or embarrass him in front of his peers by misbehaving. He took great pride in what he did and in his standing in the community. He was in the Moose Club, the Jaycees, the American Legion, and the Masonic Lodge, so that tells you something about him. My friends had a healthy respect for him as well. Twice a year my father served as the chaperone on our church youth group trips. The kids liked him; they sensed his interior wasn't as hard as his façade. Still, they knew not to mess with "Marshal Roberts."

Professionally, my father was responsible for transporting prisoners, serving warrants, and chasing fugitives. Among his many adventures, he once arrested Johnny Cash. One of his most significant assignments came when he was detailed to go to Dallas on November 24, 1963, to help transport Lee Harvey Oswald from the local police headquarters to a county jail. He and some other marshals were waiting in an underground garage for the police to turn over custody of Oswald, but before that could happen Jack Ruby shot him in the stomach. From that day on my dad was convinced that President Kennedy's assassination was a Mafia conspiracy.

My father's attitudes were a function of his time and place and job. He worked in the South, and he had a cop's foul mouth and tough disposition. He thought nothing of using the n-word. For instance, I vividly remember how fond he was of the man who worked as a janitor at Memphis's Clifford Davis Federal Building, where my father worked most of his days. He would give him his cast-off suits. "He's just a good old n——," my father would say, as he gathered up his coats and slacks. "Salt of the earth." Even then it didn't sound right to me, but I never thought to challenge him until the first time I brought Sean home. Sean was aghast. "He can't say that word in front of me," Sean said.

I was so inured to it that I replied, "What word?"

But my father was liberal minded in some ways, too. As with every U.S. marshal who served in the Deep South during the 1960s, he was on the front lines of the civil rights movement and he did his duty. Marshals enforced school desegregation, and in September 1962 they served as James Meredith's protectors when he registered at the University of Mississippi amid a race riot. Robert F. Kennedy proudly displayed a dented marshal's helmet on his desk in the attorney general's office, honoring the marshals' role in enforcing civil rights. My father went to Montgomery, Alabama, to take on white mobs and he did his part to provide protection for black schoolchildren.

I don't recall that my father voiced much of an opinion on the civil rights movement, one way or the other, except that he always favored law and order. He resented both sides when they spat in his face on the battle lines and he tried to shelter us from the riots and the violence as much as he could.

That became impossible in April 1968, when Martin Luther King Jr. came to Memphis to support sanitation workers who'd gone out on strike. On the day that Dr. King delivered his "I've Been to the Mountaintop" speech at the Mason Temple, my mother was in St. Joseph's hospital after undergoing a hysterectomy. The following evening, shortly before seven o'clock, there was a buzz of activity at the hospital's emergency room: Dr. King had been shot at the Lorraine Motel in Memphis. He was pronounced dead soon after being rushed to the hospital.

My father knew immediately what effect King's assassination would have on the streets of Memphis. As a wave of rioting and burning swept the city, he hurried home. He was afraid it wouldn't stop until the city had turned to ash.

I'll never forget my father coming in the house that night and strapping on his shoulder holster, while he talked calmly but urgently to my grandmother. "Miss Cummings," he said, "I want you to take the kids and drive to Jackson. I'll follow you as far as the Stanton exit, and then I think you'll be fine." He loaded us in the car and escorted us for about thirty miles on the highway, until he knew we were well out of the city.

My parents, like most of the people we knew in Memphis, were sickened by the assassination of King. I can remember the adults talking about how purposeless the death of such a peaceful, God-loving man was. Even though I was just a child, I felt the turbulence of that time acutely, partly because it affected our family life. The community was in lockdown for the next few days, and Dad wouldn't go downtown to visit my mother in the hospital without wearing his gun.

✣

Duty was always pulling my father away from us and putting him in dangerous situations. I don't remember seeing him ten times over the course of the year after Dr. King was killed. He worked constantly, called away on details whenever there was fresh unrest, a death threat, or a bomb threat. Much of what he did was to enforce court orders. He also protected local judges and stood guard at courthouses where unpopular judicial decisions were issued.

One of those decisions was handed down in Memphis a few years later when a federal judge infuriated the white community by ordering that our school system be integrated by busing. The judge, Robert M. McRae, received telephone death threats. Guards armed with rifles had to be stationed outside his office, and U.S. marshals, my father among them, were assigned to guard his home and courtroom.

For several years the Memphis school board had willfully resisted desegregation. After Judge McRae's order, tensions rose across the city. An action group named Citizens Against Busing angrily called for a boycott, and every white politician in the city, including the mayor, backed them. As the rhetoric escalated, there were fears of racial violence, and thirty-three leading citizens signed an advertisement pleading for calm and urging respect for the law.

The court-ordered busing plan—issued in January 1973— called for shifting 13,800 students to different schools, and it directly affected me. At the time I was attending a middle school called Wooddale, a perfectly homogenous institution in our East Memphis neighborhood. But, under the new plan, I'd be bused across town to Hamilton, an all-black middle school over by the river.

My father immediately pulled me out of the public school system. He had very strong ideas about race and about which neighborhoods were safe and which weren't, so much so that I was forbidden to go to certain parts of town. He wasn't alone. There was a massive white exodus as parents deserted their schools. In the month of January, 7,532 children were withdrawn. As an emergency response to busing, Citizens Against Busing opened twenty-six "education centers," most of them in temporary classrooms leased from churches. Some families even moved out of Memphis to counties where their children could still attend segregated schools.

My friend Tammy Scott's father was a public school teacher and he insisted that he was perfectly fine with sending his daughter to Hamilton. But Tammy's mother put her foot down—she was too frightened by the busing issue. Thousands of other parents made the same decision, though some—like my parents—cited safety rather than segregation. But whatever the rationalization, the simple fact was that many of the whites in Memphis didn't want their kids going to school with "them."

That spring about thirty-five thousand white students failed to register. Memphis was the nation's tenth-largest public school system, and now it was half emptied. Meanwhile, private school enrollment exploded. Before busing, there had been just forty private schools in Memphis, most of them Roman Catholic. Suddenly, there were ninety. New private schools began springing up all over.

Parents banged on the doors of the city's Catholic schools, hoping to enroll their kids or looking for information on how to set up private academies. To her credit, Sister Gwen McMahon, superintendent of Catholic schools in the Memphis diocese, was horrified. She said, "I believe the witness they are giving to children and adults and parents is very bad. I think we have to learn to live together and I don't think that setting up schools at this time in history is very Christian."

The Baptists mobilized and filled the gap. Church groups raised large sums of money for capital building plans; in no time at all, redbrick institutions appeared on sprinkler-fed lawns and white schoolchildren began filing into them. My parents enrolled me in the eighth-grade class at one of them, the spanking new Briarcrest Christian School, which was founded as a response to busing by eleven different local Baptist chapters. The school opened in 1973 with eighteen hundred students and consolidated in a new $6 million building the following year. That was where I met several people who became my lifelong friends, including Tammy Scott Folk, Donna Purcell Austin, and Lynn Blumenfeld Schaefer. We were all from the same East Memphis neighborhoods.

It's painful to say it, but Briarcrest was established as a direct result of racial fear and an almost wholesale unwillingness by Memphis whites to mingle their precious children with blacks. The irony was that a school that was set up specifically to oppose integration would one day welcome Michael Oher.

Today the devastating effect of white flight is still visible in Memphis. In 1979, the U.S. Department of Health Education and Welfare surveyed six thousand school systems around the country and found that the Memphis system was the fifty-third least desegregated. Now almost 90 percent of the children in Memphis public schools are black and 70 percent of them are from low-income families.

Schools like Briarcrest emphasized a Christian philosophy, but everyone knew what was really behind them. A "Christian education" had only become important after busing was ordered. As Louis Lucas, a lawyer who had fought hard for desegregation, said, "The interest in God generated by busing is phenomenal."

❦

Sending my brother and me to a private school was a major hardship for my parents, and it put nearly constant financial pressure on them. If I remember correctly, the tuition for each of us was eight hundred dollars, which in those days was a huge amount for my parents. I can remember my father saying, "I hope we get back enough on our income tax to pay the kids' tuition this year."

My mother found a way to pay for the extras in our family. She was a go-getter who worked all the time, a self-made and self-educated woman who held down two jobs on top of raising two children. As a newlywed, she put herself through a series of design courses at the University of Memphis and landed a job at Sears as an in-house designer. She nearly lost the position because she refused to work on Saturdays, which was her only day to be with me. Her boss said, "All our decorators work on Saturdays." She replied, "Just give me the chance and I promise I'll make more money than any of them." She did, too—in fact, she hustled until she made enough to open her own business and then she took some of Sears's clients with her. She was a tornado, a colorful twister of energy, and she always acted as if her glass was half full.

Her small shop was full of brilliant samples of fabrics, tiles, and squares of carpet, and gradually she added some antiques. She was in the right place at the right time when the condo boom hit in the mid-1970s and she did some model interiors for a new development in Memphis. That led to a number of other jobs, including a big account decorating Florida time-shares.

My mother's business was bust and boom, though. There were successful years and there were lean ones; it all depended on which cycle we were in. At times she made triple what my father did and she'd go on buying trips to Europe to look for antiques and stay at the Dorchester Hotel in London. Then there were times when the family bank account ran short and she worked evening shifts at a local jewelry store until nine o'clock. As if that weren't enough, she had to pass twenty hours of classes each year in order to renew her designer's license. But I rarely saw her tired or heard her complain.

The household accounts didn't allow much leeway for luxuries. For instance, our annual family vacation was a driving trip. We'd go to Gatlinburg or the Great Smoky Mountains, to Disney World or Panama City. We'd pile into the car and race along the hot tarmac of the freeway, made hotter by the fact that my father would chain-smoke his Winston Golds, with the window cracked open only a little to let out the smoke.

Seeing my parents work so hard made me independent early. I got my first job when I turned fourteen. I was a shop girl at the Limited for a while and then branched out to waiting on tables. (Over my college summers I worked at a Steak and Ale, and you should have seen me in that little apron.) But it was up to me to get myself where I needed to go, whether to a dance or to cheerleading practice, because it simply wasn't an option for my parents to chauffeur me around. So I applied to the Department of Motor Vehicles for a "Hardship License," which the state of Tennessee granted to minors fourteen and older in special circumstances, to help them get to school or work. I was only allowed to drive to certain destinations within a ten-mile radius and I had to pay for the gas. None of which seemed like a particular hardship to me. It just made me realize early on that I had to be mature and accountable.

Looking back on it, I think my parents must have worried about how they were going to pay for my college education. But they didn't express their concern aloud, even when I considered Baylor, which would have been hugely expensive. My father would simply ask, "Do they give money for cheerleading scholarships?" which was how I knew that the expense was on his mind. But they never put limitations on me—quite the opposite. My mother told me the only place she didn't want me to go was the University of Memphis, which would have been the cheapest option. She wanted me to get away from home and experience college life.

My mother was as expansive and sparkling as my father was flat and terse, and she still is. Her decorating style leans toward bold colors, and in her personal taste she's downright flamboyant. She's a classic southern lady who loves to dress with lots of lamé and jewelry. We're talking about someone who will wear sequined belts to church at the age of seventy.

As Collins says, "We have to reel her in." It's nothing for her to put on After 5 sling-back evening shoes for Sunday service. If I say something, she'll come right back at me: "Just mind your own business."

I learned more about interior design from my mother than I did from my formal education in the field. She was a wheeler-dealer who could go to an estate sale and spot a quality antique in disrepair, a diamond in the rough. She would redo it, and a week later it would wind up in someone's house. She was also one of those people who could glance at a room and do the mental calculations for the needed materials off the top of her head. She could size up exactly how many widths she needed for drapes and how many rolls she needed for the wallpaper. They don't teach you that in school—I use a calculator to run the little formulas I learned in my design courses and half the time there are errors, because the formulas don't take into account a room's idiosyncrasies.

My mother is my partner in Flair I Interiors, and whenever we have a difference of opinion or quarrel over a job, I tend to lose. We'll argue over some furniture or fabric, and I'll say, "I'm the one with the degree."

She'll shoot back, "I'm the one who's worked for forty years."

I have no answer for that because it's the truth. She *has* worked her whole life and she's still working.

❧

Despite my family's financial struggles, the only thing greater than my mother's capacity for work was her generosity. She opened our house on Sunday afternoons to all our friends, feeding them fresh vegetables and homemade peach pie. She hosted a Bible study class at our home for high school girls and volunteered as a counselor on church trips.

She was always mothering strangers, people outside of our immediate family. My sophomore year of high school, we took in an exchange student from Japan through a Christian mission program. By the end of the school year, Hideo Sumaie had become so attached to my mother that she said, "I don't want to go back. I'd really like to stay another year." My mother just said, "Of course, you're welcome to," and so Hideo lived with us for a second year.

My mother also had a habit of looking after stray kids. She became a second mother to my friend Liz Marable, who eventually ended up living with us virtually full-time. Liz was really the first Michael and she jokes about it now. "If I was black and athletic," she says, "there could have been a movie about me, too."

Liz was one of six kids from a broken home and her family had very little money. Her mother also struggled with various emotional burdens, so finally Liz moved in with her grandmother. But her grandmother was blind and ailing with diabetes and a series of strokes meant that she spent a lot of time in the hospital. Liz would stay with other families when her grandmother wasn't able to care for her and our house gradually became Liz's mainstay.

Liz went to a public school near Briarcrest, and we met through church socials. Then we both wound up at Ole Miss, which is where we became close friends. She was a rusty-haired girl with ruddy cheeks and, at nearly six feet tall, she was a phenomenal athlete who earned a scholarship to play basketball.

As a junior varsity cheerleader, I often saw Liz play; we got the less prestigious events like women's basketball, while the varsity got to be on the sidelines at football and basketball games. But I loved our Ole Miss women's team, which was coached by a future Hall of Famer named Van Chancellor, who would later win four WNBA titles and an Olympic gold medal.

As friends, Liz and I were a strange mismatch. I was tiny and blond and chattery; she was very tall and quietly sensitive. But we shared a sardonic sense of humor and we always found something to laugh about. One thing about her puzzled me, though: whenever I tried to bring her home for the weekend, she would always make an excuse and decline.

It turned out she was in awe of my stylish, cyclonic mother. Other girls often turned to my mother as a confidante, because she was a sympathetic counselor-chaperone. But Liz was wary of her and almost seemed to go out of her way to avoid her. Liz didn't want to get close to her, and I finally came to understand why: she feared her own yearning for a mother. She had never had a lot of affection and, although she craved it, she couldn't count on getting it. So she dealt with her fear by staying away.

Finally, I dragged Liz home with me one weekend. Like most college kids, we'd brought duffle bags full of dirty clothes with us, and my mother offered to wash them for us. That was when she realized how little Liz had. She was sorting a load fresh from the dryer and saw that Liz's bra was so old that there was barely any fabric left. Most of the rest of Liz's clothes were almost as threadbare.

My mother was having a good year in business and she offered to take us to lunch at Colonial Country Club, which had a nice buffet. When I told Liz we were going to lunch at the club, she said, "Okay, I know what a country club is, or at least I've heard of one. But I've never been to a country club. What am I going to wear?" I thought about that for a second and ran downstairs to talk to my mother.

A moment later I sprinted back up the stairs. "Don't worry about the country club," I told Liz. "We're going shopping— Mother and I are going to take you."

We went to the old Goldsmith's department store, a Macy's-like institution where Memphis ladies had been shopping since 1870. (When I was young, Goldsmith's ubiquitous jingle was "All about the south.") That day, my mother spent nearly five hundred dollars on a new wardrobe for Liz. She bought her skirts, blouses, and shoes. Liz tried things on with a dazed expression on her face—no one had ever bought her so many clothes at once. My mother even picked out some new sets of bras and underwear.

Later Liz would joke, "She didn't just dress your outside, she dressed your underneath side."

That was the weekend we began making Liz a part of the family. We never formally said, "You're going to be Virginia's daughter and Leigh Anne's sister." We simply opened the family circle and welcomed Liz into it. It started with sleepovers and shopping trips and grew from there. But when it came to physical affection it took a long time for Liz to overcome her reserve with my mother. For about two years, whenever my mother would try to hug her, she would shy away.

Liz had the same fear Sean and I would later recognize in Michael: she was afraid my family would eventually leave her. She worried that she was setting herself up to get hurt, that we were just being good Christians and didn't really love her, that our interest in her was temporary and would fade. But we never went away; we were in her life for the duration.

Years later, when Michael was talking with Liz one day and wondered aloud why we took him in and whether my affection for him was real, Liz just shrugged and told him, "It happened the same way with me and *her* mom thirty-plus years ago."

That's not to say that Liz didn't sometimes find our whirlwind ways a real challenge. To me, quarreling was part of being a family. I have a big voice and I'm opinionated. I have a way of pushing people—not out of anger but out of love. Once, when we were in college, I caught Liz drinking in a popular bar in Oxford called the Library. She was sitting with some of her basketball teammates and sipping a kamikaze. Now, I knew she came from a long line of alcoholics—it was in her genes. So I came up behind her, grabbed her by the hair, and jerked her right out of her seat, hollering at her the whole time. Next, I asked her to go to church with me.

It took a while for Liz to get used to being barked at. She'd get her feelings hurt and then wouldn't say a word to me.

I'd say, "Why won't you talk to me?"

At first she wouldn't answer but finally she'd say, "Because you hollered at me."

But I barked and hollered at everybody. I'd holler at her and then two seconds later I'd say, "Where do you want to eat?" It would give her whiplash.

"Didn't I just have a big argument with you?" she'd ask.

"No, did we argue?" I'd say, oblivious.

Now we just love each other and go on. It's the way we live in our family: we laugh hard, we cry hard, we win hard, and we lose hard.

※

The most interesting thing about my family's relationship with Liz is that she has passed it on. We adopted her; in turn, she's practically adopted half the city of Memphis. After she graduated from Ole Miss, she got her master's in education and became a teacher and a basketball coach in the public school system. She's now taught and coached here for nearly twenty-five years.

Liz has a contagious passion to better kids' lives. Her attitude is that we've got to stop looking at underprivileged students' weaknesses and look at their strengths. That's not to say you don't work on a kid's deficiencies, but we've got to show more confidence in them and their capabilities. So many people say, "I would love to do something but I don't have the money." But Liz Marable has never had money. She just has optimism and a tremendous faith in kids.

When I ask her what keeps her teaching in the Memphis public school system when the failure rate is so high, she answers, "Because I know it could be higher." Liz borrowed a quality from my mother: she takes each kid personally. She's helped scores of them land scholarships—and in the case of Celeste Willis, she did far more than that.

Celeste was a seventh grader on one of Liz's teams and the daughter of a single mother from the Memphis projects. One night in 1990, a neighbor armed with a gun tried to break into their apartment. Celeste's mother wrestled with the intruder and the gun went off, killing the neighbor and wounding a seventeen-year-old girl who was in the hallway. Celeste's mother was charged with murder, and her public defender failed to mount an adequate defense or mitigate the charge. Celeste's mother got life and she was sent to the Nashville Penitentiary, where she served just a few months before she was murdered in a jailhouse fight. At thirteen years old, Celeste was an orphan.

Liz took Celeste into her home, at first temporarily and later permanently. She foster mothered her through middle school and high school and then sent her off on a basketball scholarship to Union College in Jackson, Tennessee. (It killed us when Celeste turned down a scholarship to Ole Miss!) Her teams won two national championships and she earned the nickname "Baby Barkley," after Charles Barkley. She even made it to the WNBA, where she spent a few months playing professionally. After that she went back to school and got her master's in education.

Celeste is now a teacher herself and she's a model to a new generation of kids at White Station Middle School in Memphis. She's also the mother of three: Jalani, and twins Laila and LeBron (who are named after Laila Ali and LeBron James).

Liz likes to brag that she's a grandmother. "And, boy, are we an athletic bunch," she says, laughing.

Help me out here: does that make my mother a foster great-grandmother? I don't know, but when my mother recently helped Celeste decorate her house, including the kids' rooms, they were all part of a big, very happy family.

That's how infectious giving is.

My friends and I were always one dollar short in college, but nobody cared. We were too caught up in the romanticism of Ole Miss, with its Greek revival columns and sheltering three-hundred-year-old oaks and magnolias. My four years were a haze of sorority rushes and formal balls, the frantic blaring and pacing of marching bands, the drawling yet sharp-witted voices of Kappa Delta sorority sisters, the smoky humidity of tailgaters in the Grove, and a succession of friends whose faces seemed always flushed by fun, heat, liquor, or ardor.

> Are you ready? Hell yes! Damn right!
> Hotty Toddy Gosh Almighty!
> Who in the hell are we—Hey
> Flim Flam Bim Bam
> OLE MISS BY DAMN!

We always made the most of our weekends, but by Sunday evening we had spent our allowances and were pretty much tapped out. We might have just enough money to buy some vegetable soup at the local Holiday Inn, but sometimes even that was too expensive. One Sunday when we were down to our last buck, my roommate Tammy Folks and I hit on a creative way to raise funds: we collected the recycling coupons from all the tampon boxes we could find in the sorority house and took them to the drugstore for the refund. We walked out with a roll of bills and feasted on cheeseburgers.

Kappa Delta was the go-getter sorority at Ole Miss: we were cheerleaders, homecoming queens, and student body presidents. We hardly ever lost a campus election and we had a lot of dates. Tammy claims she had trouble juggling all the phone calls from my suitors, but I only had five or six, including the quarterback of the football team and the captain of the male cheerleading squad.

Then came Sean. I'd made varsity cheerleader as a sophomore and I was doing the Hotty Toddy and climbing on human pyramids—I was in the middle row—when I first noticed him. It was during our big upset of Alabama, when he went to the free throw line with a second left to hit the game-winning shot. While he was shooting I thought, "That boy sure does have good-looking legs."

That night at the Kappa Alpha party I introduced myself in my rather high-spirited way. Shortly afterward, I sent him an invitation to a KD "crush" party, an affair in which we all invited someone we liked from afar. The invitees didn't know who had summoned them and wandered around the room waiting to be flirted with. Sean, Mr. Phi Delta Theta, figured out pretty quickly who had invited him, and it wasn't long before he also figured out I liked him for himself, not because he was a big-shot ballplayer.

Although I was aware that Sean was a campus hero, I didn't know much about basketball—I was too busy bounding around on the sidelines doing back handsprings. What I did know was that I was instantly attracted to him, and the attraction strengthened once we got to really know each other. We'd set out on a date and wind up talking until five a.m. We'd talk about faith and values and what we wanted to do with our lives. We fell deeply in love, but I also came to really *like* the man who would become my husband, and I still do.

For all the joking about my outspokenness and strong personality, there's no question that Sean had a greater influence on me than I did on him. When we were younger, we came at things from the opposite perspective: I was going to tell you what was wrong with something, but Sean was going to tell you what was right with it. In time, he tempered my judgments and made me think harder about the effect of my words before I spoke.

"You can run people over with a bulldozer," he'd say, "but they don't necessarily survive it."

Sean wasn't judgmental and he helped me see that I was sometimes too quick to judge. He always saw someone's worth. He would say, "You just don't know what the guy next to you has going on. He may have mud on his shoes or a tattoo, but you can't judge the worth of that person just by looking at him."

Everybody was equal in his eyes. As he still says, "Everybody starts on the same page and we're all going to end on the same page."

As a ballplayer, Sean was showy, physically cocky, maybe even a little arrogant—he had the confidence of a lifelong great athlete. But he was also quietly and incredibly smart. Oddly, he didn't care to act like it, which was another reason I was attracted to him from the start. It was almost as though he was testing you, to see if you could figure out what a keen intellect there was underneath the jock and the charming southern boy act. Personally, I've always considered him brilliant. And I don't use that term lightly: I think he might be even smarter than his younger brother Seamus, who has a PhD from the Massachusetts Institute of Technology.

Even in college, Sean had another appealing trait: he had a way of making me *seem* in charge, even when I wasn't. He maintained the pretense that I made the decisions and he was just along for the ride. He joked that he never won an argument.

We'd bicker about something and he'd say, "I'm not going to win. But if I can get to a tie, I'm taking it. I'll call that a victory."

When we were juniors, I demanded that he throw away the old rugby shirt he wore every day. He graciously agreed and then let me take over his wardrobe. He also turned over his money to me. Athletes at Ole Miss got grants, tuition, and meal stipends, whereas cheerleaders didn't quite get a full ride. I insisted that Sean hand over the checks.

Sometimes we used the money to eat, but sometimes I used it to pay for my clothing before the bill got to my mother. (I had to dress well because I was on the homecoming court as well as Miss Sorority, so occasionally my needs outstripped my mother's funds.) Finally, I asked Sean to put my name on his checking account, and he did.

When Tammy heard about that, she said wryly, "He was probably scared not to."

But, truth be told, Sean was the driving force in our relationship, right from the beginning. He was the gentle giant behind me, the stronger one. I knew we were heading toward marriage the summer after our junior year, when he asked that I come to New Orleans to see his family. Liz and I drove down to the Gulf Coast, and she joked that I kissed a boy in every town on the way from Memphis to New Orleans. Really, I only kissed one in Jackson, as a sort of consolation.

❦

Sean and I spent our senior year enjoying Ole Miss idylls and plotting our lives after college. While we waited to graduate, Sean considered his career options. Fortunately, he had impressed an Ole Miss patron named George Lotterhos, Collins's future godfather. Lotterhos steered Sean to an investment bank, which offered him an entry-level position. Sean accepted, but before starting at the bank he had to pass the Series 7 and Series 9 financial certification exams, which are the required tests for anyone who deals in securities. Sean was about to leave for Europe to play summer-league basketball, but the firm warned him that the tests were difficult and he would need to stay home and study. Sean said, "Nah, I'll just take 'em now." He took them both on the same day and passed. That's Sean.

We had planned to enjoy one last escape by traveling together in Europe before we started our working lives. But then Sean's father got ill, and soon we found ourselves growing up a lot faster than we wanted to as we coped with the unanticipated sadness of his dad's death.

What's more, my own once-strong parents were having a hard time. Their marriage failed; their temperaments were ultimately just too different. My father faced mandatory retirement from the U.S. Marshals Service at the age of fifty-five, and his postretirement years would be sickly and unhappy. Years of heavy smoking resulted in heart disease: when a doctor drew a picture of his heart and colored in the part that was still healthy, it was just one little area. My father moved back to Jackson, Tennessee, and I would often drive over to see him on the weekends. He'd tease me and say, "I'd have gotten sicker sooner if I knew my kids would come around." In 1997, at the age of just sixty-six, he would die of a massive heart attack.

These were just some of the realities we confronted as we began married life. We had a nest egg of a thousand dollars, which we had borrowed from my parents, and three thousand dollars Sean's mother gave us for a downpayment on a house. Sean's starting salary was just eighteen thousand dollars a year, and I found a job working in the sales department of a small letter courier service. We agreed to wait to have children; we knew it would be a few years before we could afford a baby.

Still, Memphis seemed to us to be full of opportunities. The city was a thriving crossroads of bridges, iron tracks, and boat wakes, at once a railroad freight hub and the second busiest cargo port on the Mississippi. It was a center of commerce and entrepreneurship, home to several Fortune 500 companies—including one named Federal Express, which was growing swiftly thanks to our friend Fred Smith, the founder. It had great charter schools and was becoming a nexus for medical research. And the city had great atmosphere, from the bluesy strains of Beale Street and the smoked taste of barbecue, to the damp, muddy smell of that great brown Mississippi River coursing through it.

Memphis also had its problems, both tangible and spiritual, from polluted brownfields to crime. (At the time, it was rated the fourth most dangerous city in the country, a statistic that's still argued over.) And with a population that was 62 percent black and 32 percent white, it still had sharp racial divisions. But the city was filled with good-hearted people who were phenomenal givers and who could fashion innovative solutions to intractable problems. All in all, we couldn't think of a richer place in which to raise a family.

Life was a test, Sean and I agreed. God wanted to see how we would deal with various circumstances. That was why He gave us our problems, pleasures, assets, and deficits. It was why He made people black, white, Latino, and Asian; why people were wealthy, poor, and middle class.

It was all part of the Big Test, and one of the questions on the test was, "What do you do with difference?"

God gave us problems to see how we would handle them. And He gave us difference to see if we could learn to live with one another.

INTERLUDE

Sandra Bullock

ACTRESS

LEIGH ANNE SCARED ME FROM THE MINUTE SHE OPENED the door. I just sat in a chair in her house with my hands folded in my lap. I couldn't say anything. I mean, you don't meet an energy like Leigh Anne's *ever.*

I still don't know how to describe her. She doesn't care what prisoners she takes in her quest to do what she has to do. She manhandles quarterbacks and sasses football coaches. She barges in on school principals. She'll grab me by the face if she needs to. In some people, that sort of aggression might be off-putting, but she uses her energy for good. She offends some people along the way, but too bad. People need to get out of her way.

For the longest time, I kept saying no to the role, because I didn't know how to play this woman. Here she comes from Memphis, this white, Christian, Republican lady, whose bark and voice is so strong. I'd passed judgment on the southern Christian ladies. I would just roll my eyes at them. I kept telling the director, John Lee Hancock, "No, this is not going to work for me." I didn't know how to approach it or what I could bring to it. Then John said at one of our meetings, "Why don't you just come meet her?" He could not explain Leigh Anne to save his life.

I agreed to do that and went to Memphis. I spent the whole day with her, about eight hours, and I left there completely exhausted. I was intimidated by her but I was also intrigued by her, and by the end of the day I wanted to make sure that I left on her good side. Because you don't want to be on Leigh Anne Tuohy's bad side.

I said to John, "Now I know why you can't explain her, because she's original."

The biggest obstacle was my distrust of organized religion. People use their faith or their religion as a banner and then they don't do the right thing. They go, "I'm a good Christian and I go to church, and this is the way you should live your life." We're so quick to tell people how to live. I always felt like, "Do not give me a lecture on how to live my life when I know I'm a pretty decent human being. I might not go to church every day, but I know I try to do the right thing, whereas you're going to church and you're still sleeping around on your wife and spending everybody else's money. How are you better than I am?"

I told Leigh Anne, I said, "One of my concerns is the whole religious banner thing. It scares me because I've had experiences that haven't been great. I don't buy a lot of people who use that as their shield."

But she was so open and honest and forthright. Her love is so big, and they found their third child because of it. Here's this family that had the instincts to say, "This is what we're going to do, we're going to give love and reach out a hand," and they had no idea that they would get a son in return. People questioned them, of course. We don't trust anyone who does anything nice. But they didn't care and they kept going.

There was such a bond between those people and their children that you wanted to pay homage to them. I realized, "Wow, I've finally met someone who practices but doesn't preach." So I've had the blessing of having my . . . not a restored faith, but I now have a faith in those who say they represent a faith. I've finally met people who walk the walk and it's made me really happy. It makes you feel like you need to step up your game.

I don't know at what point I said yes. I don't recall. I don't think I ever said yes, I just got pulled into it. I felt a great sense of fear in trying to tackle this dynamic person, but also a great sense of obligation to be true to her. If I was going to play Leigh Anne Tuohy, it was going to be an inspirational, true-life story with the message that we're capable of so much more than we think we are. I was scared enough to say, "If I'm going to do this, I need to prepare for it. Let me get to a place where I can make Leigh Anne Tuohy real, rather than someone who's this cartoon version of a steel magnolia." Which I think it easily could have become.

Once, when we were driving down to Ole Miss, I asked her if it was true that she carried a gun. She said, "Yeah." And then she reached over and opened up the console—and pulled out a pistol.

I just said, "Oh dear God."

The great thing is, we get to play these people and get to experience lives that we normally would never come in contact with. "WWLAT do?" That's what I would say on set. "What would Leigh Anne Tuohy do?" Everything I wore was what Leigh Anne wears. Every design label was what Leigh Anne would wear. Every bit of makeup was from her palette. Her watch was her watch.

I constantly tell her, "This is your story, it's not my story." She has no idea the path she's begun, in terms of adoption and fostering. I don't think the Tuohys realize the profound effect that they are going to have, what they are going to do for our country in terms of making people aware of this problem. It's not been on the forefront of people's minds, but it is now. It is on the forefront of *my* mind now, every day, when I get up. I look around and I go, "Is he? Is she? What is their situation?" And it's because of this family.

3

The Two-Penny Gift

LEIGH ANNE AND SEAN

A person's true character is judged by how he acts and reacts to someone who has no consequence in his life whatsoever.

—SEAN TUOHY

OUR FIRST HOME WAS A TINY COTTAGE IN A SECTION OF Memphis called Sherwood Forest, where all the streets had names out of Robin Hood. We lived between Maid Marian Street and Friar Tuck Lane, and the rooms were so cramped we joked that you could sit on the commode and make the bed, stick your feet in the bathtub and cook dinner—all at the same time. When our first cousin and dear friend Judy Edwards came over to see the house for the first time she said, "Oh, my gosh. Is this the whole thing?"

We just nodded.

She flicked her eyes around the house, which amounted to less than eight hundred square feet. You had to pass through the bathroom if you wanted to get from one room to another. Judy tried to find the right polite words to hide her dismay. She failed.

"This is a serious setback," she said.

Sherwood Forest was an East Memphis subdivision of about twelve hundred colonials and brick starter homes, relics from the late 1940s and early 1950s with metal awnings and cheap siding. It had originally been intended as a neighborhood for working-class whites: the covenant approved by the Memphis Planning Commission back in 1946 prohibited "any race other than the white race" from occupying the structures except for "servants' quarters." Now the area was mixed, with a lot of retirees, but we all had the same thing in common: nobody made more than thirty thousand dollars a year. Our mortgage was $391.72 a month—which is now our cable bill.

We renovated the house ourselves, with the help of our friends. Judy, who would become S.J.'s godmother, worked tirelessly to make that little place special. Sean opened up some space by taking down a wall with a hammer and then he announced that he would repaint the living room, which was an unattractive teal green. This was on a Saturday, but it happened to be the Saturday of the Georgia-Florida football game, and after several hours and three pizzas he had only painted about eight feet of wall. Leigh Anne walked in and said, "You're fired."

Our furniture came from garage sales; we'd buy old pieces and refinish them ourselves. The crowning touch in the living room was a large painting of a Chinese man, which Leigh Anne bought from her mother. Sean swore it gave him the creeps because the man's eyes followed him when he walked through the house. "That guy keeps looking at me, every day," Sean said, and finally he covered it. So our wall art was a picture with a towel over it, though we did remove the towel for company.

After less than a year Sean gave up the investment bank job; even in a bullish market he didn't like to call people he knew and ask them for money, so he decided he wasn't cut out for it. Peter Willmott, the chief financial officer of Federal Express, sat on the board of a small company that sold home alarm systems, and Sean took a job with them. He liked to joke: "I went from securities to security."

For twenty-two thousand dollars a year Sean employed his talent for ignoring how-to manuals by installing alarm systems. He strung the wiring himself, crawling on his belly under porches, and stooping beneath the eaves of dusty, mice-ridden attics. (On only his second job, he fell through a rotted attic floor into a lady's bedroom.) He fought off raccoons, rats, and ten-inch-long snakes, which he seemed to believe were ten feet long and so deadly that if they touched you, you would die.

He worked ten hours a day and he came home covered in grime, with bug bites under his eyes. He was on call around the clock and slept with a walkie-talkie by his bed. But he liked the work a whole lot better than sitting at a desk trying to talk people into giving him money. He could take apart an entire alarm system and put it back together and he didn't believe anyone could do it better.

Leigh Anne showed a knack for business right from the start. The only woman in her department, she hustled all over town in a used Cutlass and peddled an overnight messenger service. She outsold everybody. Nobody should have bought a thing from her, since she was a competitor in the town where FedEx was founded, but somehow they did. Sean cracked that her sales pitch was "Use my service or I'll come whip your butt."

We were hardly getting rich but we soon discovered that we had more in our pockets than a lot of people. An early lesson in the power of giving came with just a twelve-dollar price tag. In 1984, Liz Marable began teaching math and coaching girls basketball at Treadwell High, a faded old redbrick edifice serving about 850 students that was made famous by Penny Hardaway, who had played basketball there.

Teaching was all Liz had ever wanted to do. "I just want to work with kids," she said. "I don't want to work with adults because I don't like us that well."

Over dinner one evening, Liz told us that there were eight kids in her class who couldn't afford to get their annual physicals. A basic medical checkup cost just twelve dollars, yet their families didn't have the money.

Impulsively, Leigh Anne blurted out, "We'll pay for it."

It was a reflexive response. Medical checkups were a necessity and the tab amounted to only ninety-six dollars. That's all it would take to do something vital for those children. It seemed like the steal of the century—if you had a hundred dollars, that is.

Liz replied, "You'll pay? I'm helping you pay *your* bills! How are you going to pay for it?"

Somehow we found a way to foot the bill, and it wasn't too painful. Pretty soon we found ourselves doing more. A few months later, Liz called us one Friday morning and mentioned, "I've got a kid who's going to a funeral this weekend, and he doesn't have any money to buy decent clothes." That afternoon Sean went shopping and picked up a pair of slacks and a blazer for the boy, because he knew what it was like to feel shabbily dressed.

When Leigh Anne saw the receipt, she thought, "Are we going to have enough money to pay the light bill this month?"

The bills kept coming, as they always do. We didn't have much—and we didn't always give cheerfully, or without worry. Sometimes we hoped that good intentions counted as much as the dollar amount.

❦

It took four years of grinding work before we felt secure enough financially to think about a child of our own. Sean was promoted to president of the alarm company and he also began making some money on the side in sports radio. Leigh Anne's sales bonuses were so strong she was pulling in forty thousand dollars a year. Between the two of us we could pay the mortgage each month and not have to worry about the lights or heat getting cut off.

Collins Tuohy was born on December 29, 1986, and that was the day the world really started spinning for us. It was a long, tough delivery; Leigh Anne was in labor for nearly twenty hours. She was in so much pain afterward that she had trouble walking. But for all of the difficulty Collins had in making her entrance, she was the easiest baby in the world once she arrived. She had an utterly angelic temperament.

The nurses put her in a Christmas stocking, and for the

first few hours her grandmother Virginia held her and would not give her up. Finally a nurse came in and said, "Only one person can be in here with the mother at a time."

Virginia and Leigh Anne just turned and looked right at Sean. After a long moment of dead silence, he said, "Okay," and stood up, leaving the three generations of Collins Cummings women alone.

Collins was such a perfect baby that at first she slept twenty out of every twenty-four hours, and during the four hours when she was awake she gazed placidly at the ceiling. Occasionally she would make a small ladylike noise, her way of suggesting she'd like a bottle. When she got old enough to hold one herself, we would place the bottle in a corner of her baby bed. She would wake up and take a drink and then place it right back where it was supposed to be and doze back off.

Our friends were furious at us for having such a sublime, effortless infant. At church they started prayer circles for us, and this was the prayer: "Please, God, let their next kid be rotten so they will appreciate the difficulty of parenthood."

Collins was a deal breaker for Sean. He was working too many hours and he decided he didn't want to miss any time with her. The clincher came when she was two years old and appeared in a children's Easter play—Sean almost had to skip it because he was supposed to be on call for the alarm company. He had to go to his boss and ask for permission to take the afternoon off. He walked out of the office thinking, "I'll never do that again. I don't care if I have to dig ditches in my own backyard."

He decided he had to be his own boss. He didn't mind working ten hours a day, but from now on he wanted to pick the ten.

Sean started looking around for entrepreneurial opportunities. In early 1988, Leigh Anne's brother Stanford came across a Taco Bell franchise that was for sale in Meridian, Mississippi. Sean and Stanford put together a small investment group that included Stanford's father-in-law, and they bought the franchise. They designated Sean the group's managing partner and named their little corporation Ole Bellco, as a tribute to Ole Miss.

A couple of times a week Sean began commuting 230 miles to Meridian, with the goal of making the business such a success that he could decide his own hours. He got up at five o'clock to dice a couple hundred tomatoes and onions. He learned to do amazing things with a knife. He cleaned the industrial dumpsters himself, shoveling out the garbage and spraying them down. One day early on, he came home and told Leigh Anne, "That was one of the best days I've ever had—because it was my dirt, no one else's. I owned it."

When two more Taco Bells became available, Sean and Stanford bought them using the capital from the first one. Soon Sean was putting in sixty hours a week running the franchises. He had gotten lucky and latched on to a good brand and he was in a great position to grow the company. At the age of just twenty-six, he was on his way to becoming a fast-food baron.

❦

At last, for the first time in our lives, we were financially comfortable. But where money was concerned, we were a contradiction as a couple. Sean spent almost all of his time trying to make money, but Leigh Anne woke up every day looking for ways to give it away. It was a race to see whether Sean could buy something before Leigh Anne could pass the cash on. Whenever we had some extra money, Sean would say, "Hey, how 'bout we give some of it to me?"

We didn't know how much we gave and we didn't track the percentage. Sean would tell friends, "I just give what feels good—or what's left, because Leigh Anne usually gives it away before I get there." Leigh Anne also liked to spend money on herself. Teasing her, Sean would say, "You don't have a closet, you have inventory."

But we both agreed that along with a larger income came larger responsibilities. One of our favorite sayings was from Luke 12:48: "To whom much is given, much is required." Leigh Anne put it more informally. "God gave us what we have to see what we're going to do with it," she said. By the early 1990s, as we realized we had a chance to become wealthy, we began to think more formally about giving and how to do it most powerfully.

Neither of us talked very openly about our faith, because we didn't want to offend or alienate or preach at people. We attended the nondenominational Central Church led by Jimmy Latimer, the pastor who had married us. Jimmy delivered simple but powerful sermons, and his frequent readings from the Bible, with an emphasis on the Ten Commandments, was a new experience for Sean, a departure from the Hail Marys of his boyhood Catholicism. Perhaps for that reason, Jimmy's reading of the Bible affected him more deeply than any reading of it had before.

It was around this time that Sean, with a fresh set of ears, heard Jimmy Latimer deliver a preaching tour de force on the true nature of giving that lasted for four straight Sundays. Jimmy could be that rare combination of funny, serious, and honest in his sermons and he was all of those things on the subject of giving. When most ministers talked about money, they got a little self-conscious; there were simply too many huckster preachers in the world who lived high off collections from worshippers. Usually when Sean heard a cleric scolding his congregation or urging people to put more in the plate, he clenched up. He began squirming in his pew seat and thinking, "Oh, here we go, he's hitting me in the wallet."

During the first of those four sermons on giving, Jimmy was aware of some tension in his audience and he addressed it sardonically. "I know I'm going to run people off with this, but it's what I need to talk about and I'm going to do it," he said. Because he was so honest about it, Sean sat a little straighter and paid more attention.

First, Jimmy explained the real meaning of the term "cheerful giving": he said that it's what we feel in our hearts when we grasp the depths of God's generosity to *us*. We receive countless gifts, starting with sun and wind. "Yet he did not leave himself without witness, for he did good by giving you rains from heaven and fruitful seasons, satisfying your hearts with food and gladness"(Acts 14:17).

So many people believed that they created and owned their own wealth, and they felt no obligation to give much of it back. But, as Jimmy reminded us, the Bible teaches that God owns everything and allows us to keep it for Him. He asks only that we be responsible stewards and that we voluntarily tithe a small amount. Jimmy further explained that the Old

Testament word "tithe" actually translates to mean 10 percent. Was that really too much to ask?

Sean had never known the meaning of the term. *I can go for that*, Sean thought.

What's more, we shouldn't begrudge money that went directly to the church, Jimmy said. In the Book of Malachi, the Bible talks specifically of how we are to give to our local communal "storehouse." Why shouldn't we all share in the maintenance and upkeep of the community, and especially church facilities, since we all used them?

"Next time you need to bury your grandmother, try calling some guy in Tulsa and see if he'll come and do it," Jimmy said.

Finally, Jimmy suggested that there was a purpose to tithing beyond mere church maintenance: it was a way to get our hearts right. In fact, the decision to give away at least 10 percent of our income affected our whole outlook on life. It meant sacrifice, living a little more frugally ourselves, consciously passing up on personal luxuries in order to give to someone and something outside ourselves. In that sense it was an exercise in unselfishness. It forced us, on a weekly basis, to place importance on others.

Tithing taught us to sacrifice as cheerfully as the widow who gave the two-penny gift in the Bible. She surrendered her last two coins, and they were treasured by Christ because she had so little.

> And he sat down opposite the treasury and watched
> the people putting money into the offering box.

Many rich people put in large sums. And a poor widow came and put in two small copper coins, which make a penny. And he called his disciples to him and said to them, "Truly, I say to you, this poor widow has put in more than all those who are contributing to the offering box. For they all contributed out of their abundance, but she out of her poverty has put in everything she had, all she had to live on" (Mark 12:41–44).

By this point Jimmy had worked himself up to a good, old-fashioned fire-and-brimstone pitch; he was really rolling. Now he drew himself up for the grand conclusion. His voice deepened, his tone darkened, and he thundered: "And if you *don't* give . . ."

Pause . . .

"God will bust you!"

Sean hung on every word; it made more sense to him than anything he'd ever heard. He started tithing that day—that very day. He loved the sermon so much he also went to the church bookshop and bought a cassette tape of it, so he could listen to it again. He started putting it in his tape player when he drove back and forth to Meridian to oversee the Taco Bells. He played it over and over again, as if it was a favorite song.

No sermon or homily had ever resonated quite so much with him. For one thing, he liked the utilitarian aspect of it: if you could be happier about writing a check, it just made for a better day. After all, what was the happiest day of the year? Christmas, of course. Why? Because it was the one day of the year when the whole country gave cheerfully.

As Sean listened to the sermon while driving down the highway, he began evolving his own personal philosophy of giving. He wanted to do more than merely tithe. He wanted to have a cause. But he also wanted to be sure that the money wouldn't be wasted. The more he thought about it, the more he realized that giving wasn't simple—it could actually be quite complicated.

✿

By this point in our lives, both of us were thinking a lot about giving, and we began having lively discussions about it. What was the right way to give? Should you give money to a guy begging on a street corner when you knew he'd just buy whiskey with it? Leigh Anne said no. "There's a difference between giving and enabling," she said. It was a good point, but Sean wasn't so sure.

We were continually solicited, and the range of choices could be bewildering. Friends asked for donations to their favorite charities—Red Cross, United Way, Save the Children, and many others. Pleas arrived through the mail and came over the television set. A press of people asked for support, from the alumni office at Ole Miss to kids raising money for a class trip. Were we supposed to give a little bit to everyone? Or just one large amount? Should we give aid overseas or give only to Americans?

"To give away money is an easy matter and in any man's power. But to decide to whom to give it, and how large, and when, and for what purpose and how, is neither in every man's power nor an easy matter." Aristotle said that and it makes as much sense now as it did two thousand years ago.

If we weren't careful, we could start comparing causes as if they provided return rates on investments. And the uncertainty about which cause was most deserving could lead to paralysis or irritation. Pretty soon we'd wind up feeling guilty about all the ones we said no to. We might get discouraged and decide we couldn't make a big enough difference. We might just shut down and complain, "Everybody's always got a hand out." Or, when we did finally give, we might do it cautiously, grudgingly. Which was not cheerful giving at all.

In the end we decided that we too often confuse the *power* of giving with the *effectiveness* of giving. Giving was powerful by itself; it needed no help from the recipient to be meaningful. Giving worked on the giver's heart and made it expand; that was the most important thing. What the recipient did with the gift—whether he used it to change the world or buy whiskey—was up to him. If what we gave went down a hole, then that was on the head and heart of the person on the receiving end of the gift. God would judge his heart, and that was *His* responsibility, not ours.

As Sean put it, "My responsibility is to be happy with the act of giving, without expecting a result."

We decided that if we waited until we were fully informed about where our money was going, if we insisted on being entirely comfortable with what it was spent on, we'd never give nearly as much as we wanted to. It was sort of like having a baby. If you waited to be "prepared," you'd never have one.

❦

Sean Junior was born on July 4, 1993, despite Leigh Anne's best effort to deliver him on a different date. It had taken her a while to agree to have a second child, because Collins's labor had been so painful. Also, as much as she loved kids, Leigh Anne wasn't big on babies. They made her nervous; they couldn't talk and tell you what they needed. Leigh Anne was a fixer and she was more comfortable once kids could tell her what was wrong. Collins would point at a scrape on her elbow and say, "It hurts," and Leigh Anne would look at the cut with relief and say, "I can fix that." If Leigh Anne had her way, kids would come out of the womb at age twelve, so that she could do their hair properly and make their clothes match.

Leigh Anne went into labor with Sean Junior at about nine o'clock on the night of July 3. Her obstetrician was a friend and a former Kappa Delta sister named Diane Long. Diane promised to make the delivery easy—once a KD, always a KD. But Leigh Anne's contractions were accompanied by a case of severe irritation, because the chances were excellent that the baby would be born after midnight, on Independence Day. That meant there would be a lot of silly festivities and carrying on over the baby at the hospital. Leigh Anne didn't want a bunch of tacky Fourth of July baby pictures, with stars and stripes in the background.

She told Diane and the nurses, "I'm going to have this baby *tonight*. I don't want to deliver this baby on July fourth and have you hand it to me wrapped in an American flag. I do *not* want cheesy pictures of this baby in bunting."

Sean just stood by her side and said calmingly, "Sweetheart, I don't know exactly how this works, but you better start howling and pumping and pushing if you want to get this baby out before midnight."

Friends and family began streaming into the hospital. The

room filled up until a crowd was packed three deep around Leigh Anne's bed. It looked like we were hosting a barbecue—we practically had an open bar. Then our pediatrician, Dr. Bill Fesmire, arrived. He was another good friend; his wife, Karen, was also one of Leigh Anne's Kappa Delta sisters, and their daughter Maggie was Collins's best playmate.

Dr. Bill practically had to fight his way into the delivery room. When he saw the crowd he said, "Wow, I've been to parties with less people."

Sean and Dr. Bill got tired of fighting the throngs, so they sat down in a corner and played games of Spades, while Leigh Anne breathed in and out and tried to hurry her contractions so she could deliver the baby before midnight.

But the hour came and went. No birth. "Well, good try, sweetheart," Sean said. "It certainly was a commendable effort. You gave it your best, but you just couldn't do it."

Leigh Anne glared at him.

Sean Junior finally arrived at about two a.m. No sooner had he entered the world than, just to aggravate Leigh Anne, the nurses cleaned him and swaddled him in a cute little American flag. He looked like a tiny parade float.

But the joy of S.J.'s grand entrance was tempered when Dr. Bill said, "He feels hot." It turned out that he was born with a fever; he had something called a Beta Strep infection, which can lead to pneumonia or meningitis, among other scary things. S.J. had to be treated with antibiotics immediately, so they ran an intravenous tube into his neck. We had a tense night, and then several more anxious days, waiting for reports from specialists before we knew that S.J. was all right and we could bring him home.

Leigh Anne as a toddler on the lap of her mother, Virginia Cummings Roberts, who gave her warmth, an eye for color, and the motto, "Don't talk about it. Live it."

Leigh Anne's father, Stanley Charles Roberts, stole his brother's birth certificate to enlist in the army at seventeen and was decorated in the Korean War.

The Roberts family qualities were all on display in this domestic portrait: Stanley's toughness, Virginia's flair, Leigh Anne's personality, and baby Stanford's mischief. In the background is the car in which we took the family vacations.

All photographs courtesy of the Tuohy family unless otherwise noted.

Sean's mother, Mida, was from a socially prominent New Orleans family, but she chose to marry a gym teacher and never had a bad day while he was alive.

Sean's sister Sarah, who loaned him his first car, a Vega with all the horsepower of a broken-down mule.

Ed "Skeets" Tuohy was a tough Irishman from Chicago, but he was also the greatest dad in the world.

Skeets Tuohy wanted his sons and basketball protégés (from left to right, Edward, Seamus, and Sean) to play the game fast, slick, and without thinking.

Sean stood on top of the world after leading Ole Miss to the 1981 Southeastern Conference basketball title. He still holds the conference record for assists. Note the blood on his chin and knee. The jersey he wore hangs over son S.J.'s bed.

Virginia Roberts always found a way to pay for extras, such as this gown Leigh Anne wore to a tailgater in the famed Grove as a member of the Ole Miss Homecoming Court in 1981.

Sean escorted Leigh Anne on the football field at Homecoming in 1981. She picked out his clothes—he was always very coachable where she was concerned.

We were married on June 12, 1982, in a five-thousand-seat Evangelical pulpit in Memphis. Leigh Anne had proposed; Sean simply obeyed.

Leigh Anne and her mother partner in the interior design business, while her brother, Stanford, partners with Sean in his restaurants.

The perfect child, Collins Tuohy, holding her equally perfect though somewhat less accommodating younger brother, Sean Junior, on a beach in Destin, Florida.

Our three children in the backyard in high school (from left to right): S.J., Michael, and Collins. The first time Michael spent the night, S.J. said, "Who's the big dude on our couch?"

A triumphant senior night for Michael and Collins at Briarcrest High School's Clayton Field. He was one of the top recruits in the country; she was Homecoming Queen and state champion in the pole vault. S.J. wore his basketball gear because he had dashed to the field straight from a game. The rest of us were just proud.

Photograph by Dana B. Goode

S.J. on the baseball diamond for Briarcrest. "Watch your blind side!" the hecklers chant at him.

Michael and Collins became inseparable at Ole Miss. Our cheerleader daughter and football-playing son integrated that old southern campus in a way no one had quite seen before. "I thought ya'll were twins," one of Collins's friends said.

The Tuohys on their way to a family wedding in March 2009, looking for once the way Leigh Anne wishes they did all the time. The expression on her face says it all.

Michael and Leigh Anne savor the moment after the Baltimore Ravens selected him in the first round of the NFL draft. "I had dreams about the moment, years before," he said later.

Sean with his friend and impersonator, Tim McGraw. We both married women way above our heads.

Sandra Bullock's sass fit right in with the girls in our family.

Mister and Missus Tuohy go to Hollywood. We did not observe proper decorum at the Oscars. This was our most sedate moment.

✿

Our children became the second great romance of our lives. We lived for our kids; we were perpetually entertained by them and loved them to distraction. But from the beginning, we were in firm agreement that they shouldn't be the center of our lives. We wanted our children to be a *part* of the family but not the nucleus. We set out to teach them that the world didn't revolve around them. Rather, they were a piece of a larger puzzle, members of a community—whether their church, their athletic team, their Boys and Girls Club, their neighborhood association, or a family reunion.

We set clear rules that were calculated to help them understand that. First of all, the marriage bed wasn't for children. Collins and S.J. never slept in it with us, ever. We stuck by that and it served us well. When they were infants, they slept in cribs in our room, but as soon as they got old enough we moved them to their own rooms, at which point a second rule went into effect: neither of them were to enter the master bedroom without knocking and receiving express permission. We believed the bedroom was our sanctuary. If they were sick, one of us slept in their room with them.

We also believed that once a child went down for the night, they were to stay in bed. This was easier to enforce with Collins, who was the perfect child, than with Sean Junior. Shortly after we moved him to his own room, he began to try to get out of his baby bed. We had a video monitor in his room, so we could see him drinking his bottle. Then we'd hear a thunk as he tossed the bottle on the floor. Next, we'd see him throw a little leg or arm over the bed's railing and try to climb out. Leigh Anne would go in there, take the bottle away, and tell him to lie down. He'd cry and want to get up.

This went on for a while until finally Leigh Anne called Dr. Bill. He told her not to give in: she should just shut the door and let S.J. cry it out. Pretty soon, Dr. Bill assured her, he'd stop trying to get out of bed. "It's going to be the worst couple of nights of your life, but you'll be so glad you did it," he said.

The next two nights were torture. S.J. wailed for hours at a time. Leigh Anne looked at Sean with tears welling up in her own eyes and said, "I'm not listening to that anymore."

"You've come this far," Sean told her. "Don't give in now."

She didn't—and S.J. finally stopped crying and stayed in his bed.

We were very strict: we practiced zero tolerance. If you asked Leigh Anne what her parenting style was, she'd say, "Fear and repetition." There was no right or wrong to it—it was just our personal philosophy that strictness at a young age would preempt a lot of problems later.

We believed our children were capable of learning obedience as early as eighteen months. We taught them a few non-negotiable rules as preventative measures. For instance, Leigh Anne knew that scissors were a source of fascination for small children. One of the reasons she knew that was because she had taken a pair and whacked her own ponytail off at the age of five, requiring her first and only pixie cut. Virginia had cried for a month every time she looked at her. Leigh Anne didn't know what a pixie was, she just knew her mother wept every time she heard the word.

Collins had exquisite long hair, and Leigh Anne didn't

want a repeat of the hair trauma. So she sat Collins down on the floor, held up a piece of paper in front of her, and began to cut it with scissors.

"This is what you do with scissors," she said. "If you ever do anything else with scissors, *I will take away everything you have.*"

Collins had a little doll that she was particularly attached to. To be doubly sure Collins got the message, Leigh Anne held up the doll solemnly. "You use scissors to cut anything but paper? You will never see her again."

That wasn't really true, but the point was driven home. There were no hair incidents with Collins.

In our house, we never put anything up out of our kids' reach. We left the Limoges boxes and other knickknacks out. We didn't want to clear all the objects from the coffee tables and hide them from the children. With each child, it took several weeks of constant attention, and we spanked their little hands until they were red, but they learned not to disturb anything in the living room.

The kids would tell you that we didn't parent them so much as brainwash them. Collins was still a toddler when Sean taught her his favorite college fight songs. Sean would play tapes of school anthems to her in the car on the way to nursery school. It got to the point where she would dress her doll while humming "Cheer, Cheer for Old Notre Dame." By the time she was in grade school, she could name every university in the Southeastern Conference and also name their mascots.

Church was another nonnegotiable. If a kid was too tired to get up and go to Sunday service, then the penalty was the suspension of all their voluntary activities. "If you're too tired for church, then you're too tired to do anything else the rest of the week," Leigh Anne told both of them. We didn't permit them to treat worship as it if was less important than cheerleading practice or basketball practice or a dance.

We also didn't allow their things to become obsessions. They had a time limit for certain toys, such as the Xbox. Each evening around nine thirty, their cell phones were confiscated and put into the laundry room, because that was the rule.

"It's not that I don't trust you, I'm just taking the temptation away," Leigh Anne would say. "When you get older you can make your own decisions, and then it will be up to you whether you want eight hours sleep, or want to be stupid and stay on the phone until two a.m. and suffer the consequences of being tired and getting sick."

Our kids were in bed by eight thirty or nine, as soon as their homework was done. Collins swears that the only TV she ever saw at night was a half hour of *I Love Lucy* reruns. If we did have something on the screen, it was usually a game. Sean was fascinated with sports of all kinds—it didn't matter what language or what country, if they kept score, Sean watched it. Until, one day, Collins walked into the game room, and Sean was watching cricket. "We have to draw the line somewhere," she said. "Cricket and bowling, we're not going to do."

Privacy was another zero-tolerance issue. Our children had no rights of privacy at all. "When you're on your own, paying your own rent and your own utility bill, then you can have privacy," Leigh Anne would say. "But when you're in our house, there are no locked doors."

Also, Leigh Anne was perfectly cold-blooded when it

came to searching their drawers and closets for contraband. She told the kids, "Everything that's yours is mine. I get to look at everything you have." Collins was perfectly amenable to this, being Collins. But S.J. was a little less so; he tended to want to close his door. Sometimes, he did it just to see Leigh Anne get prickly and hear her say "Open the door *now.*" She reserved the right to go through our kids' drawers, their bags, their cell phones, and their cars. She'd search under the seats and in the glove compartment and she didn't apologize for it.

"Information," she'd say, "is a valuable tool."

❦

We also didn't believe that kids should have idle time. There was no coming home in the afternoon and getting on the computer and obsessing about video games. Whether it was playing in the band or appearing in a school play, our children were going to do as many things as we could enroll them in. The one thing they *weren't* going to do was be a slug.

We piled after-school activities on their plates until they hardly had a free moment. Collins was in gymnastics by age four, and then she added piano, swimming, track, and cheerleading. S.J. played basketball, baseball, and golf, studied piano, served as a volunteer basketball coach for a group of younger boys, and wrote for the school paper.

We wanted them to be on sports teams because we believed in the values that went with it: discipline and dedication. If nothing else, they had to be on time and responsible to others. In gymnastics, Collins worked on four different apparatuses with very little margin for error. She'd practice until nine o'clock on Friday night and have to be back in the gym Saturday morning at eight. The sport was demanding on her body and it left her with almost no free time, which was what we liked about it. She actually became a Level 9 gymnast—which means she was potentially Olympic caliber—but she finally gave it up when a coach suggested she needed to move to Houston and participate in an elite program. At that point she switched to cheerleading.

We've always had a hard-and-fast rule that our kids either participated in sports and after-school activities or got a job. For instance, S.J. loved basketball but he wasn't as enthusiastic about baseball, and one afternoon he announced he wanted to give it up.

Leigh Anne said, "Well, fine, then you can go work somewhere."

"What do you mean, work somewhere?"

"You're not going to sit home and play Xbox, S.J., you're going to go find a job."

"Mom, I'm in seventh grade. Where am I going to get a job?"

"Well, your father owns a Taco Bell."

We also insisted that our children take music lessons once a week. We didn't care if they played the kazoo; learning a musical instrument is a discipline and a good experience to have, and we wanted them to at least give it a try. It wasn't an option.

Neither was quitting. At sixteen, S.J. decided he hated the piano. One day he announced that he didn't want to play anymore.

"Fine," said Leigh Anne. "Then you can't play sports, either. And I'll take your car."

"Okay, I'll keep playing piano."

Once he realized that girls liked to hear him play, S.J. started practicing more often and began to actually enjoy it.

Behind our insistence that our kids learn an instrument was the fear that we were a little too sports crazy and that the kids needed some broadening. But with Collins, Leigh Anne might have carried the efforts to make her a well-rounded young woman a bit too far.

By the time she got to high school, Collins was an incurable jock. She was a medal-winning gymnast, a city champion in freestyle swimming, a triple jumper, and a state champion in cheerleading and pole vaulting. Not only was she incredibly talented, she was hugely competitive.

"She'll rip your heart out, step on it, and *like* it," Sean boasted. "Oh yeah. She is a Tuohy when it comes to competition."

But Leigh Anne decided Collins needed to balance her athleticism with something ladylike. She came up with an idea that Collins found nearly diabolical: she made her enter a Junior Miss pageant. Leigh Anne thought competing in Junior Miss would force Collins to learn how to carry herself in an evening gown, handle a public interview, and perform on the piano before an audience.

Collins begged not to do it. She pleaded. But Leigh Anne was unwavering. She took Collins shopping and bought a full-length black Oscar de la Renta dress. She also picked up a head-to-toe mirror at Wal-Mart.

On the day of the competition, they set up the mirror and Leigh Anne helped Collins dress, while Leigh Anne's dear friend Debbie Branan stayed backstage to help Collins between events. Collins had heard that one trick competitors used was to put hair spray on the bottoms of their new shoes so they wouldn't slide. Since Collins was a gymnast and a pole-vaulter, she had a can of Stick 'Em that she used on her hands for grip. She decided that if hair spray was good for shoes, Stick 'Em would be even better. "I'll use this," she thought. She shook the can and started spraying—and got the stuff all over her gown.

It looked like it had snowed on her dress. Collins leaped up and stared in horror at the hem of her gown. She lunged to the full-length mirror to look at herself—and in the process tripped and knocked the mirror over, shattering it. Standing there, with goo all over her gown and shattered glass at her feet, Collins lost it.

"Puh-leese don't make me doooo this!" she wailed, her voice hitching. "Puh-leese!"

Leigh Anne calmed her down. "You're going to be fine. You're going to walk across that stage and be fine."

And she was. She paraded across the stage, sat down at the piano, and ran the keyboard, performing "How Great Thou Art," one of her great-grandmother's favorites. She nailed the piece. She had arranged it herself for the special occasion, and it awed the crowd. It was her last public performance as a pianist.

※

As the kids got older we gave them more independence and let them make some of their own decisions. Our attitude was that we trusted them 100 percent—unless they screwed up. But the rules remained strict at night. They were to sit in the center of a movie theater, because nothing good happens in the back row of a theater, just like nothing good happens after midnight.

We didn't let the kids go to parties unsupervised by parents, and we personally checked up on them.

When Collins was in the seventh, eighth, and ninth grades, Sean would drive her to dances or parties and sit outside in the car until she was ready to leave. It meant a lot of nights behind the wheel listening to the radio or leafing through *Sports Illustrated*, but that way she knew her dad was out there whenever she wanted to leave. When she turned sixteen and was old enough to drive, we finally let her go to parties alone. Oddly, Sean found he missed those evenings. The first time she went out on her own, he said, "It's kind of sad that she's out there all by herself—I'm not there if she needs me."

When S.J. was invited to a friend's house for the evening, Leigh Anne always called the parents and said, "You will be there, right?"

On one occasion, the mother replied, "Well, actually, we thought we'd run to the movie and let the kids have the house."

Leigh Anne said, "Well, then I'm sorry but he won't be able to come over tonight. I'm just not real comfortable with him being in someone's home without parental supervision."

The mother got real quiet and then said, "Oh. Well. Wow. This is the first time I've ever been told that a kid can't come over."

Leigh Anne said, "Please don't change your plans because of us—he can come over another night."

Thirty minutes later the mother called back and said, "We're going to stay home. We really want to. And thank you for calling and being so honest about this."

Our final edict concerned academics: we strongly preferred

that our kids didn't bring home tests or report cards with Cs on them. As and Bs were the only grades we wanted to see. When they were little, we had tried to establish the right habits by spending hours going over spelling words, working through math problems, and checking their homework. Fortunately, they both proved to be good students. Collins had to work at it, but she became an honors student. S.J., on the other hand, didn't have to work hard at all and he still made As. We didn't know how he did it, because the books never seemed to come out of the backpack and we never saw him do much homework. Yet to date he has only got one C in his life, in one grading period of honors geometry.

When Leigh Anne saw that grade, she was not happy. But as far as Sean was concerned, it was a case of "Do as I say, not as I do." He couldn't bring himself to upbraid S.J. about that one C—he was elated by what a good student S.J. was.

Leigh Anne glanced at Sean and saw that he was smiling ruefully.

"I can't take this on, sweetheart," he said. "I ain't ever made a four-point-oh if you added two semesters together. So don't look at me—this one's yours."

❧

Our kids didn't get allowances. "Food and a bed, that's my allowance," S.J. told people when they asked him how much his parents gave him each week.

So no allowance, and no vote either—because kids shouldn't get votes. But when Collins and S.J. totaled up the deficiencies in their childhood, we hoped they'd mention the swimming pool in the backyard.

By the late 1990s, Sean and his partners in RGT Management were on their way to acquiring more than eighty Taco Bells, Long John Silver's, Pizza Huts, and Kentucky Fried Chickens spread across Tennessee, Mississippi, Kentucky, Ohio, and Missouri. At the same time, Leigh Anne's design business was thriving, thanks to athlete clients from the Southeast who had made it big in the NBA and NFL and had called her to decorate their new homes. It didn't hurt to have a good friend in Memphis named Jimmy Sexton, one of the most powerful sports agents in the country, who represented a vast array of coaches and athletes.

Wealth didn't just present us with a moral dilemma, it also presented us with a parenting dilemma. How could we give our children every advantage and yet not spoil them rotten? We couldn't hide our income from our kids—we had a million-dollar house and six cars for four people. We liked our stuff; there was no doubt about it. Leigh Anne collected so much David Yurman jewelry that Sean teased, "I thought I was buying stock in a company. It just keeps amassing."

Meanwhile, to make the commute to his restaurants easier, Sean acquired a private plane, a small twin prop with leather seats that could comfortably seat eight people. He dubbed it Air Taco.

So we didn't exactly deprive ourselves and we couldn't pretend that we didn't enjoy spending money. But we could stick to certain principles. We could give generously and hope the example would teach our kids to give as well. We came up with a philosophy we called "Get One, Give One." It was sort of a one-in, one-out theory. When we got something, we had to give something.

Albert Einstein said it well: "It is every man's obligation to put back into the world at least the equivalent of what he takes out of it."

We tried to show our kids that little things add up and we started in our own closets. Much as Leigh Anne liked her clothes, she believed hoarding was a sin. She'd tell Collins, "If you haven't had it on your body in the past year, I want it in a plastic bag so we can give it to someone who will use it." Every few months we made our kids go through their closets and take bags of stuff to Dress for Success and the Neighborhood Christian Center.

For every privilege we had, we tried to make Collins and S.J. give something in exchange for it. Like most kids in our neighborhood, they went off to summer camp, but in their case they started at a place called the Camp of the Rising Son down in Choctaw, Mississippi, which was a camp for underprivileged kids between the ages of seven and sixteen. We wanted them to get a dose of reality, so that they wouldn't be too sequestered by comfortable circumstances. It was a wonderful starter camp that was real and relaxed, and they did what kids at camp always do—they splashed around in a lake, did arts and crafts, and had campfires. But they came home with a sense that they had it pretty easy compared to some children.

When Collins got older she wanted to go to a camp called Kanakuk, an expensive, high-end extreme sports camp in which kids learned white-water rafting and climbing. We were fine with Kanakuk, but we urged her to do something in exchange, some activity that involved giving back.

Collins decided to go on a mission trip to Guatemala, and she spent over a week there. First she helped build a cobblestone road to a small, inaccessible village and then she carried sandwiches into the Guatemala City dump, where people lived amid the refuse and scavenged every day for subsistence. At first Collins couldn't believe her eyes: the dump was a huge canyon of landfill and garbage, and scrambling around inside of it was an entire colony of people.

Thousands upon thousands of people squatted on the rim of the landfill. They prowled through the garbage, combing it for glass, or cans or plastic, which they sold for just thirty cents a kilo. They built homes from discarded scraps of tin and cardboard—and somehow had the spiritual resilience to fill those sheds and lean-tos with expressions of faith and hopefulness. Collins came home with searing images in her head: of crucifixes and pictures of Christ hung on corrugated shed walls, of babies in diapers crawling in the piles of trash.

Our aim in exposing our kids to such things was not just to make them more observant and more sensitive to other people's needs but to show them where their giving ended up. It wasn't enough to give to a blind trust. Collins could have mailed a check to a relief effort in Guatemala and never seen those kids living in garbage, but then she wouldn't have given anything of herself. Working in that dump made her responsible for the giving.

※

Many of our friends became role models for our children. Over the years we made donations to their various causes: some years a basketball team needed new sneakers or uniforms, other years we sponsored trips to summer youth camps. We hoped that through our kids' connections to these people, they would see the end results of giving, which would make them more interested and invested in it.

We wanted to get to the point where giving became its own reward and we wouldn't have to push our kids to help others. To begin with, though, we had to force them to do certain things. We were under no illusions: children are inherently selfish organisms and they have to learn to see beyond their own small dramas and urgencies. It helped that Briarcrest put something of an emphasis on outreach. Each spring the school had a Great Day of Service. The campus closed down and each class performed volunteer work, whether raking an elderly person's yard or cleaning the pantries at Ronald McDonald House. Anything to teach them that not every child had a mother, father, two cars, a cell phone, and a laptop.

Initially, we had to push S.J. to volunteer for Bridge Builders and for the Big Brother program. "This is really not optional," we said. "There are some things in your life that aren't optional."

When he turned fourteen, we got him a hardship license, and he began driving across town to Ross Road Elementary School, where each week he met with and mentored a fourth grader. Ross Road is in one of the more crime-ridden neighborhoods in Memphis, and initially we were reluctant to let him go there alone. So, for the first three or four trips, we followed him and sat out in the parking lot, just to be sure he knew how to get there and showed up on time. Finally, Leigh Anne said, "This is one of those things where we're just going to have to trust God."

Our parenting method seemed to work: although S.J. was certainly used to having what he needed and wanted, he wasn't evolving into a selfish kid. He knew there was another world beyond the comfortable one he lived in and it bothered him. At some point we realized that he no longer had to be told to do things for others; he did them on his own. When a kid on his recreational league basketball team had to play in the same pair of sneakers for two summers in a row, even though they had gotten too small for him, S.J. noticed it. The next time we bought S.J. sneakers, he asked if we could buy some extra pairs.

He also noticed when a new kid in his class didn't have a dress-code necktie. Every Wednesday the boys at Briarcrest were required to wear neckties to chapel. S.J. couldn't tie a necktie properly yet, so we'd tie one for him and hang it on a loop in his closet. He had two revolving ties. Each week Leigh Anne would go through his backpack, pull out the used necktie, clean it, retie it, and hang it back up. She is all about parts and pieces: if you leave the house with certain parts and pieces, you are required to return home with them.

One Tuesday night Leigh Anne was getting S.J.'s things ready for chapel and she could only find one tie in his closet. She went downstairs like a bull in a china shop, yelling.

"Sean Junior! Where did you lose your tie?"

He just sat there and let her rant and rave.

Then he said, "Are you finished?"

"Yes."

"One of the kids on the team didn't have the money to buy a tie. I had an extra one and I gave him my tie."

Leigh Anne can be very gracious in defeat. "Okay," she said meekly.

❧

Long before Michael Oher came into our lives, Collins and S.J. learned to accept the presence of other kids sleeping on the sofa. Children who didn't have what everyone else had always tugged at Sean's heart, so the house was full of his protégés.

When Collins was in seventh grade, Sean drifted into coaching. He began to hang around the Briarcrest gym to watch her cheer and his eye would wander from his daughter to the boys playing ball. What he saw was simply not good enough. The Briarcrest seventh-grade boys won just two games that year—Collins was a much better cheerleader than any of the boys were players. At the end of the season Sean went to the administration and said, "All right, if I've got to go to every game, we're going to get a lot better than this." He volunteered to coach the eighth-grade team and the school accepted.

Coaching proved to be one of the most satisfying things he had ever done. The first time the kids called him "Coach Tuohy," he stopped and looked around for his dad. It was like hearing the sound of a beautiful bell. What's more, he discovered he was pretty good at coaching: a team that had been in the basement did an about-face and won twenty-eight games and only lost their local championship game in overtime.

At the same time that Sean was becoming involved in coaching, Briarcrest embarked on a drive to admit more minority students. Under a wonderful headmaster, Tim Hillen, and principal, Steve Simpson, the school instituted a scholarship and financial aid program through which kids could help offset some of their tuition by working at the concession stands or cleaning up after games for an hourly wage. But the program needed funding. At that point tuition at Briarcrest was about

$8,500 a year, and some families who received financial aid still found the cost prohibitive.

The idea spoke to Sean's old point guard instincts: as someone who had once "assisted" with basketball passes, he appreciated it when he saw the principles of assistance in action. There were lots of good people at Briarcrest like Hugh Freeze, coach of the varsity football and girls' basketball teams, who wanted to make sure that kids had options if they couldn't afford the tuition. How could we deprive kids of opportunities over a little money? As parents at a Christian-based school we felt charged by God's word to help. "I'm here if you need me," Sean told Hugh. "Please don't let a kid slip through the cracks over a few dollars." We became contributors to the program, and Sean told Hugh he didn't care about the student's age, gender, color, passion, or interest. It gave Sean satisfaction when he went over to Briarcrest and Hugh would point out a child—a member of the band, or a girl on the softball team—and say, "That's one of the ones you're helping."

Helping out was a natural inclination for Sean—he wouldn't have gotten anywhere in life himself if his schooling hadn't been paid for by generous givers. Nor was our interest restricted to Briarcrest. Through other friends of ours—people in key positions at numerous schools, churches, clubs, and philanthropic organizations—we heard stories of children who couldn't afford application fees for ACT tests or to buy basic school supplies. We put the word out: if a kid needed help, whether it was a trip to a summer camp or a driver's ed class, call us.

Nor were kids our sole focus. It occurred to us that a lot of teachers could use some assistance themselves—*they* needed help. Sean remembered his father's method of paying bills by lottery. He heard about coaches at schools who were thinking of getting out of teaching because they couldn't afford to pay their health insurance, or electric bill, or some other basic necessity. Sean often picked up their premiums or paid some of their bills anonymously. Sean knew coaches who were so short of cash that they worked multiple jobs: they would work as valets, referee games, or take on a paper route in addition to coaching, and then catch naps in the afternoons when they could. They did all this just to get by and put their kids through school.

We weren't alone in lending some support, either. Giving friends influenced us with their own generosity. These friends multiplied every gift; they were wonderful people with whom we shared a passion for giving. Whenever we came across a deserving project, all Leigh Anne had to do was send an e-mail or make some phone calls to our friends and a flood of aid would arrive overnight. The e-mail and phone list was long— Pam and Hugh Boone, Debbie and Scrappy Branan, Alex and Trent Crowley, Marcy and Stanford Roberts, Brooke and Brian Sparks, Linda and Robert Sparks, Carolyn and George Lotterhos, Jenny and Russ Garner, and many others. They gave whenever they were called upon, and none of them ever questioned whether the cause was a good one. They simply reached in their pockets—and they usually wanted to remain anonymous.

At one point Leigh Anne heard about a Boys and Girls Club in need of video games. More than two hundred kids were vying for time on an old, obsolete electronic game station. She whipped out an e-mail to our friends explaining the shortfall and asking for contributions. Within a day, Leigh

Anne had a box of twenty games to send to the club, along with new and used controllers and charger stations. It was a perfect case of friendship multiplying a gift.

But the money was almost incidental to us. Most important was helping kick-start lives, or helping families spend more time together. Sean tutored four or five athletes each year, because he had seen too many cases of kids who gave their classes short shrift only to discover in eleventh or twelfth grade they had jeopardized their college eligibility. Sean wanted to catch them early, in the ninth grade, and get them straight before their academic performance became a problem.

We had specifically bought our house in River Oaks because it was so close to Briarcrest; we wanted our home to be the first place our kids and their friends came to when they left school. Often kids from Briarcrest would wander over to our house to spend the afternoon until someone could pick them up. One day when S.J. was about seven, he came home from school to find two strange boys monopolizing his video games.

"Mom, there are two guys downstairs playing with my Xbox. What gives?"

"We're helping them out. Be generous."

S.J. went back downstairs and watched the boys for a few minutes while they played with his toy.

Before long he just said, "I've got the winner."

❧

As Sean got deeper into coaching and sponsoring, we were reminded that giving didn't always have to be tangible. It was just as important to give passion, time, faith, encouragement, or exposure to something new. Sometimes these ways of giving meant much more than money ever could.

When Collins was a freshman in high school, she made it to the state championship in pole-vaulting, and we decided to travel to Chattanooga to see her compete. As it happened, we found that a great Briarcrest tennis player named Rawl Martin, who had trained at the famed Nick Bolletieri Academy, was playing for the state tennis championship at the local country club in town. Rawl's parents couldn't be there because his father traveled a lot on business. Meanwhile, the kids on Briarcrest's track team had never seen Rawl play tennis, much less for a championship, and they decided they'd like to be there to give him moral support.

The next morning, Sean rolled the track team out of bed and said, "Let's go, I'm taking ya'll to see Rawl Martin play tennis. We're gonna go root for him." We packed them in the car and drove over to Chattanooga Country Club. The admission was five dollars. Sean was counting heads and pulling his wallet out when one of the kids said, "Coach, put your money up. We'll all go hop that fence and save you the forty dollars."

Sean suppressed a grin and said, "Line your butts up single file and act like you been here before."

Well, that didn't quite happen. As soon as the match started they began hollering and screaming and cheering for Rawl. They would woof and fist pump every time he won a point. At the break, Sean took them all to the concession stand, where an elderly country club lady scolded them: "What a rude group you are. You're in bad taste." One of the Briarcrest kids just looked back at her and said, "You must be for the little boy who's gettin' his butt whipped. We feel your pain."

Sean tried to explain etiquette and how old tennis was, and how competitors wore all white at Wimbledon. Then he tried to explain the scoring system, how you went from fifteen to thirty to forty to deuce—and sometimes to ad, deuce, and back to ad again—and finally to winner. The kids thought that was simply ridiculous. "Why not just do one-two-three-four-winner?" they asked.

At one point during the second set one of the kids stood up and whistled and yelled, "Keep on, Rawl! You beatin' him like a two-dollar ——!"

Rawl hardly lost a point in the whole match. Afterward, he came up to Sean and said, "Coach Tuohy, thank you so much for bringing the guys. That was the best time I have ever had on a tennis court." Sean and the kids from the track team felt the same.

Buying some tickets to a high school event was a small thing for us; we didn't even think twice about it. As a sports-loving family we were always buying tickets to games of all sorts, from a state track championship to an NBA game—it was part of the fabric of our lives.

But for a lot of kids, attending a sporting event was a luxury. We were so comfortable that we had a tendency to forget that. The truth is, we were often as complacent and self-absorbed as anybody else. We got so busy raising our kids and so caught up in our work that we didn't always appreciate our good fortune. We didn't always give nearly as much as we should have.

But whenever we got too contented or too distracted by our own little problems, our friend Liz Marable would blow through the door and remind us of how much we took for granted. One evening Leigh Anne met up with Liz in the parking lot of a Treadwell High football game in order to pass on some tickets to a Memphis Grizzlies game. There were only a few cars in the parking lot and the stands were nearly empty.

Leigh Anne said, "Where is everybody?"

"This is everybody," Liz replied.

"But where are the students?"

"These are the students."

"No, I mean the fan students."

"Leigh Anne, these kids live in another world. They don't have five dollars to come to the game. And they don't have a ride to get here."

The next Monday, Leigh Anne called Liz. She said, "Hey, how many kids do you think really want to go to a game?"

"What game?"

"A football game. How many kids at your school do you think would really like to go to the next game?"

"Tons of them."

"Well, decide how you want to do that."

"What do you mean?"

"Decide how many kids you want to go to the game and let me know and I'll pay for the buses and buy their tickets to get in. And they'll need something to eat."

Liz said, "How about we take the kids that make good grades?"

That really bothered Leigh Anne—people were always paying attention to the children who were the best behaved and made their grades, but they often ignored the kids who were struggling. She said, "You can't do that. You can't leave those other kids behind."

We filled three buses full of Treadwell High kids so they could do what so many other children, including our own, took as a birthright: spend an afternoon at a stadium cheering for their school and their classmates.

✿

In 2001, we experienced something that snapped us out of our sense of complacency and restored our perspective: Sean's company nearly went bankrupt. We had been living paycheck to paycheck off of RGT Management and, although it was a handsome check, the company was carrying a lot of debt. A couple of events conspired to put Sean's business in trouble: the economy took a dive and Taco Bell went into a down cycle. Suddenly, Taco Bell was no longer the only destination for low-priced, quick-serve Mexican food; now there was competition from the so-called Fresh Mex chains and business fell off steeply. The financial picture wasn't pretty and it forced Sean to seriously consider filing for Chapter 11.

But a crisis, if you survive it, can be a healthy thing. It forces you to check yourself; it reminds you that with too much comfort, rot can set in. It reduces you to basics, to what's really important in your life, and makes you think about what's expendable and what's extra luggage. We had started out with nothing and over time we had acquired a whole lot of everything. Now we were possibly on the brink of having nothing again.

At one point, Liz asked Leigh Anne, "Leigh, are you scared?"

Leigh Anne realized she wasn't. She said, "I can go right

back to that house in Sherwood Forest and be just as happy as I ever was."

And that was the truth. Sean wasn't frightened either. "It's not like it's a real risk, because I never had anything to begin with," he said, shrugging.

Our kids were healthy and happy and our marriage was strong. Leigh Anne's business was in good shape, and Sean was beginning to carve out a thriving career as a broadcaster. In 2000 he had become the radio color analyst for the NBA's Memphis Grizzlies. In 2006 he moved into the TV booth as a color commentator alongside his partner and great friend Pete Pranica. The Grizzlies broadcast team, including Randy Stephens, Eric Hasseltine, and Rob Fischer, never put a bad show on air.

All together it added up to a solid living, though not the private plane kind.

❦

Fortunately, everything worked out in the end: Sean's lenders stuck by him as he completed a restructuring and a series of re-amortizations. For a while, the financial pressures meant that we had to curb our spending and we couldn't give as freely as we had. But we still had plenty to give, we realized, both tangibly and intangibly.

"Give what you have. To someone, it may be better than you dare think." Henry Wadsworth Longfellow, another very wise man, said that.

If we were ever tempted to question the value of doing something small for someone, Leigh Anne liked to tell the story of the starfish:

One day after a large storm, a man and a little boy were walking on the beach. They were horrified to see that a host of starfish had washed up on the sand, and now they were drying out and dying in the sun. The little boy frantically ran down the beach, throwing the spiny, star-shaped creatures back into the water. But there were thousands upon thousands of them, strewn across the sand.

The man said to the little boy, "You can't save all of them, so stop trying."

The little boy just picked up another starfish and tossed it back in the ocean.

"Well, I just saved that one," he said.

The power of one is more important than we know.

INTERLUDE

Collins Tuohy

DAUGHTER

WE COME FROM PRETTY SIMPLE MEANS. MY PARENTS started with nothing and they completely built up everything they have, so it's not like we've been spoon-fed and live in la-la land.

I remember my mom always saying, "Money is the root of all evil. It brings problems." But my dad likes his toys, so there's a balance. I said once to somebody, sort of tritely, "Money can't buy you happiness." This lady said to me, "It sure can rent it for a while." Which is pretty funny, and pretty true.

Once we became comfortable, my parents thought it was important that we realize that our life was not the norm. A lot of kids, if they didn't get a cell phone and a car by the time they were sixteen, they thought there was something wrong with their family. My mom would explain to me that what we had wasn't usual, that not everybody had cell phones and cars—or even running water and a toilet.

When I was fifteen, they sent me on a mission trip to the Guatemala City dumps. I didn't want to go but, whether I wanted to be there or not, I got a lot out of it. We went into the dumps and we saw everything. Oh, gosh, it was bad. It was awful and very eye-opening. You can get so consumed by your own little world that you forget how some people live. People don't want the bad news; it makes them uncomfortable. They go, "Oh, it's so sad," and they move on to something else, to take their minds off it. But you need to know it's out there.

My parents also sent me to work in soup kitchens. It wasn't that they insisted I be dedicated about it. They just wanted my eyes *opened* to it.

By fifteen, you understood that you could make something of who you were as a person that had nothing to do with money. "You can't buy character," my father said. I remember that being said *all* the time. He would add, "It can just as easily be taken away if you don't protect it." He made it clear very early on that what people thought of me was a big deal. "Your reputation precedes you," he said. "It comes before the actual you. And once it's gone, it's gone forever."

My parents are big on walk it, instead of talk it. One thing they feel is that in our society we place extreme values on people, one way or the other. Your value might be as a really "sweet" person or it might be as an "important" person, depending on certain adjectives or descriptions or the status people might assign to you. But my parents want to know, why is the garbage man not really important? He does something critical for our family every single day. For years, I've watched how my parents treat the guys who drive that truck up to our house every morning. They walk out and say, "Hey," and do something nice for them, maybe offer them a cold drink. They give them Christmas presents. One year it was a turkey. Last year it was basketball tickets. People make it out to be so hard. My mom says, "It's not that hard. They come at the same time every week."

My dad says, "It's easy to be nice to George Bush. But the guy who cuts George Bush's yard, that's the one you're supposed to be nice to. Because not everybody is going to be nice to him." After years and years of watching how my mom and dad treat people, it got across. You know the people my dad's a jerk to? Usually the people who think the garbage man is beneath them.

So when Michael came, it wasn't like we were adopting a black kid. We were adopting *somebody*. My mother fell madly in love with him within five minutes. I don't remember it being gradual. I think she just cared so much about him, and he knew that. And no one had ever cared.

We get asked all the time why we didn't resent the entrance of a third child. I have no idea. Probably because we both were so comfortable with ourselves, who we were, and with how our parents felt about us. I think S.J. and I feel that we have a whole, healthy family. And I think it goes back to the theory that God puts things and people in your life for a reason. Usually it's to show you a path. And this clearly was a path that our family needed to go down.

There were comments, but we honestly didn't hear as many negative ones as people might think. Those comments just slide off, because Michael is a blessing in our lives. The comments don't even sink into your skin. I don't ever remember thinking that they weighed on our minds, or hearts, or souls.

4

Passing It On

LEIGH ANNE AND SEAN

No matter what our origins, backgrounds, faiths, or traditions, we are all the same.

—LEIGH ANNE TUOHY

THE ARRIVAL OF MICHAEL IN OUR HOME PROBABLY should have been the cause of more tension—or, at the very least, the heavy footfall of a six-foot-five teenager with size fifteen sneakers should have disturbed Leigh Anne's carefully arranged interiors. But, strangely, there was never any conflict. The kids never even fought over who was going to do the dishes. Of course, we don't have dishes—that would mean we'd have to cook. It was, "Who's going to throw away the paper plates?"

It always seemed to Michael that our neighborhood was an hour away from the place where he grew up. The aptly named Hurt Village was a boarded-up, busted-windowed, gang-ridden urban project where all the parks had broken swings. The economic distance between Hurt Village and the genteel River Oaks—with its brick castles, gleaming Palladian windows, and box hedges—made the actual distance seem as wide as a gulf.

"Come to find out," Michael said later, "it's only five or ten minutes away. Depending on how you drive."

We didn't start out on a mission to adopt a homeless kid and we weren't looking for a third child. "Heck, I didn't want another one," Leigh Anne recalled. Furthermore, Sean's business was still on the rebound. It was simply a case of one thing leading to another; Michael was such a charmer that we couldn't resist him.

First of all, he was funny. When Michael began to stay the night with us, his old friends from the project would ask him questions such as, "What's it like to be in a house with white people?" He'd tell them, "There's never any food in the refrigerator because they always eat out."

Our relationship began with lunch. As a volunteer coach at Briarcrest, Sean was a regular visitor in the cafeteria, and he had no trouble figuring out which kids had empty pockets. They were the ones who might have only a bag of chips while everyone else had heaping plates. At public schools, you got free lunch. But the financial-aid kids at Briarcrest were almost always shocked to find that they had to pay for meals at their fancy new academy. Sean was keenly aware that pride did not fill a kid up; on the contrary, it kept him or her from telling anyone they were hungry and asking for help. In the fall of 2002, Sean quietly observed the sophomore Michael Oher as he moved around the cafeteria. Sean noticed that he didn't eat the same things as the other kids, if he ate at all. He looked like one of those kids for whom no-free-lunch was an unpleasant discovery. He looked like he went to school not knowing whether he would eat that day and hoping someone would buy him a meal. *Just like I did*, Sean thought.

One afternoon, a few weeks before Thanksgiving, Sean spotted Michael sitting in the bleachers watching basketball practice. Michael was still on academic probation and not allowed to play until he proved he could make his grades, and he stared at the court with obvious yearning. Sean climbed up the steps and introduced himself. "I'm Sean Tuohy. I'm Collins's dad and I'm one of the coaches here," he said.

Michael just mumbled something.

"You may find this hard to believe, but we have more in common than you might think," Sean said.

Silence. Head duck.

"For instance, what did you have to eat today?"

"I ate in the cafeteria."

"I didn't ask you where you ate, I asked you what you ate."

Michael said, almost resentfully, "I had some stuff."

It was what Sean figured he'd say. But Sean knew better—there was no way Michael had eaten as much as he wanted to. Sean said a polite see-you-around to Michael and went straight to Collins and asked if she noticed what Michael ate each day. When she said no, Sean said, "Well, buy him lunch, but don't let him know you did."

Then he went to the administrative office.

"Ya'll have a new kid, Michael? Real big kid?"

Sean didn't even know how to pronounce Michael's last name properly. It was one syllable, as in "oar."

"Look, here's my credit card," Sean said. "Put him on the lunch program. And make sure that he understands he can use it to eat as much as he wants. Forever."

✤

Of all the kids around town we had helped, whether with tuition or meals or a place to stay, we'd never met anyone like Michael. Those other kids had parents, or uncles and aunts, or grandparents, and they had a place to go. But this kid didn't even have somebody who could fill out paperwork for him. The scale of the need was much greater.

After we got to know Michael a little, Leigh Anne decided to take charge, and, as Sean says, "Leigh Anne is progressively more relentless as she attains power." After she took Michael shopping and bought him some winter clothes, she began asking questions. She didn't get any of the answers she wanted.

"Who takes care of you?" she demanded.

Silence.

It was apparent that the answer was no one. Where there should have been structure and protectors, Michael had a void. He awoke every day of his life to a profound mystery, unsure of whether he would eat or where he would sleep.

Michael had run away from one foster home after another, until child services had lost track of him at the age of ten. Most of the eleven schools he attended had seen him only sporadically. For eighteen months he hadn't gone to school at all—he'd missed the entire third grade. At his last public school, Westwood High, he had been absent for fifty-one days during the school year.

Fortunately, some people went beyond the usual fence line

for Michael; if they hadn't, he would never have come to Briarcrest and we would never have met him. A mechanic who had grown up in Hurt Village, and knew what a trap it could be, kept his eye out for kids who appeared to be promising athletes and tried to help them get out of the neighborhood. At Briarcrest, basketball coach John Harrington and principal Steve Simpson decided to give Michael a chance. Nobody else had thought big, quiet, placid Michael Oher would amount to anything, but Harrington and Simpson perceived that Michael conscientiously avoided trouble, despite the fact that it was all around him. And the boy seemed to *want* things—he had a good kind of hunger.

Once he got to Briarcrest, Michael migrated between the homes of four or five families. He'd sleep on someone's couch one night and on someone's floor another. He spent some time living with Matt Saunders, a young friend of ours who coached the wide receivers on the football team. He spent a few nights with the family of Briarcrest's kicker. He stayed most often with his football teammate Quinterio Franklin, who lived way out in Mississippi, in a trailer, where Michael slept on a blow-up mattress that would gradually lose air over the course of the night.

That fall of 2002, Michael was waging an internal battle with himself. He was in desperate arrears in every way imaginable—socially, academically, and financially. Although he was smart, he lacked some basic academic skills that other kids had learned years earlier. His textbooks were full of terms that were alien to him. The students beside him would flip open their textbooks, but Michael had no idea what page he was supposed to be on. At the end of class his teachers would give out assignments, and they clearly expected him to be able to do them on his own. *I've never done homework in my life*, he thought.

Imagine the stakes, and the pressure: Briarcrest was his one shot. "It was all I had," he said later. If he failed, he wouldn't get another. When he rode the bus and walked through our neighborhood, he saw more than just grand houses, he saw a vision of a life he wanted for himself. But if he couldn't find a way to make the schoolwork intelligible, the vision would evaporate and he'd be back in the ghetto. Michael was desperate to make it at Briarcrest, but he simply didn't know if he could. At times it seemed to him the most sensible thing was to quit.

"I wanted to learn and I wanted to be there and I knew it was good for me," he recalled. "I knew that at Briarcrest I could get looked at by colleges. But I was on probation and if I didn't get my grades up, and start to learn, and show some progress, I would have to leave. I was struggling in the classroom and it was really frustrating. A lot of the time I wanted to just go back to the city schools. I was extremely close to doing that because it was like, I just couldn't do the work. And I was in an awkward situation at Briarcrest, me being the poorest kid there. It wasn't the environment I was from. I'm from the ghetto, I'm from the city schools, I'm struggling, and I'm looked down upon. There were times I just didn't want to be there and so I wanted to go back to where I was from."

Luckily, a devoted Briarcrest biology teacher refused to let Michael fail. One afternoon she pulled Michael aside and spent two hours talking with him and going over a biology textbook. She searched his mind, trying to discover what he knew and didn't know. She discovered that Michael had a quick, absorbent intelligence and that he was trying to do the work. She realized that he had been staring at the biology textbook until he thought his forehead would crack open. But when it came to using his knowledge on tests, he hit a wall.

"I did my part, I studied so hard—I would study for hours," Michael remembered. "I knew the material. But on paper, it would seem changed around. It would be so changed, it was like I had never even seen it."

Most experts now agree that our traditional understanding of the word "intelligence" is too limited. It doesn't describe or measure the wide variety of capacities that people, especially kids, display in classrooms. Harvard University's Howard Gardner suggests that a child who learns multiplication easily is not necessarily smarter overall than a child who struggles. The second child may simply have a different brand of intelligence that needs to be accessed with an alternate approach. In fact, the second kid may even be smarter. One of the multiple intelligences that Gardner identifies is "bodily-kinesthetic," which describes people who learn better through movement and demonstration. They tend to be good at sports, dance, acting, or performing and they learn best by doing something with their bodies rather than by sitting and reading. They have great capacities for verbal and image retention and they do best with oral exams.

Bingo. Michael's teacher concluded that he was a better visual and oral learner than a textual learner. When she gave Michael an oral exam, he passed with flying colors. "I knew every bit of it," he recalled proudly.

The teacher reported to the other Briarcrest staff that Michael was more than capable of doing the work; he just needed some remedial tools and encouragement.

Instead of wondering why Michael was there, others on the Briarcrest staff began to notice how much perseverance he had. To principal Steve Simpson, Michael was like that storybook locomotive that huffed "I think I can, I think I can." He never quit trying. He was open to every teacher who tried to help him and never once complained about staying after school if it meant getting ahead. Simpson had never seen another student with Michael's combination of gaping deficits and tremendous drive.

❦

It was impossible to watch Michael struggle and not want to help him. Sean and Leigh Anne responded to him for different reasons, but he prompted the same impulse in both of them: here was a giant sweetheart of a kid just begging for a kick start in life.

Sean saw in Michael the kid he had once been at Newman, the poorest kid at a rich school. He began doing small things for Michael, the sorts of things people had once done for him. He slipped him a few dollars when they went on road trips with the basketball team. On Friday afternoons, he'd give Michael twenty dollars so that he wouldn't be the only kid with empty pockets over the weekend. In the evenings after practice, Sean would often wait around, jingling his keys, and offer Michael a ride wherever he needed to go. More often than not, Michael would want to go spend the night with his teammate Quinterio. Sean would stop at Sonic and buy Michael a bag of burgers. In the car they'd chat about how Sean had grown up in New Orleans and how it felt to be the only kid in the cafeteria without lunch money.

Sometimes, Sean would try to talk Michael out of going all the way out to Quinterio's place. "Why don't you just stay at our house?" he said. Finally, one evening, Michael clearly didn't have a place to go after a track meet. This time he accepted Sean's invitation.

S.J., who was seven years old at the time, banged into the house to find Michael sitting on a couch in the living room. No one ever sat in the *living room*. It was more than unusual; it was nearly unprecedented. The living room was Leigh Anne's personal display case for her untouchable objects. As far as S.J. was concerned, the room was pointless. It might as well have a velvet rope across it, like those rooms in museums. Yet there was Michael, resting on the couch, as still and upright as one of the items on the coffee table.

S.J. wondered to himself, *What's he doing sitting in there?* But he didn't devote any more thought to it, because he was in a hurry to get to a friend's house for a sleepover.

When S.J. came home the next day, Michael was sitting downstairs again. Only this time, he was on a more comfortable sofa.

S.J. walked upstairs to find Leigh Anne.

"Who's the big dude on our couch?"

"That's Michael—he stayed with us last night. He's going to study here today and go to practice with your dad later on."

S.J. did what he always did when strange kids came to the

house. He walked back downstairs and spoke the universal language of sports and electronics.

"You play basketball, huh?"

"Yeah. You?"

"Me too."

Pause.

"You like Xbox?"

"I haven't played a lot but I like it."

"Why don't we play right now?"

One thing led to another. A night on the couch became two nights. We got the feeling that Michael strategically rotated where he would stay. He'd spend a couple of nights a week in one place, but he didn't want to wear out his welcome so he'd leave and go back to Quinterio's.

Eventually Michael began hanging around our house for longer stretches. As he said later, "Every time I went to their house, it was where I wanted to be." He just felt comfortable with us, and we felt the same. He would play games with S.J. for hours at a time, until Leigh Anne began introducing Michael as "Sean Junior's best friend."

We didn't ask him a lot of questions about his circumstances at first, but we could tell that shelter was a continual issue for him and so was food. Leigh Anne would take him shopping, and afterward they'd stop at McDonald's. Michael would order three or four burgers plus sides. It was obvious to Leigh Anne that he was either taking food to other people or saving it for himself so he would have something to eat later.

To the rest of the family, it was clear that Leigh Anne had fallen in love with Michael in about five minutes. He needed mothering and she responded reflexively. They had an instant rapport. She spoke her mind to him and demanded the same from him.

With other people he was self-conscious, but Leigh Anne didn't permit that. "*Look* at me!" she'd say.

"Being around her, it was kind of crazy," Michael remembered. "It was just like she knew the ropes with me already. She wasn't afraid of anything. Some people think something and don't say it out loud. But she was going to say it, that's what made her different."

They were an odd couple, each of them the opposite of who they appeared to be. Michael was a big, silent kid whose grim, muscular exterior cloaked a gentle, amiable personality. Leigh Anne was a petite, talkative, outwardly soft woman with an inner ferocity. They quietly amused each other. You could see that in the way Michael's eyes would light up when he talked with Leigh Anne, or in the way she would look at him and purse her lips and then her dimple would start to deepen.

"He thinks Mom is funny," Collins noticed. She was right: sometimes when listening to Leigh Anne, Michael's huge frame would start to tremble with laughter. He found her alternately hilarious and completely nuts, but either way he enjoyed her.

When it came to neatness, they were utterly kindred spirits. Michael charmed her by making his bed. ("How does a kid make his bed up every day when he never had one?" Sean asked, mystified.) He would iron the shirts she bought him every morning. He would Windex the glass top of the dining table after we ate takeout. The rest of us would get up from the table and toss cartons in the garbage, but Michael would stay behind and spray the glass and then polish it, while Leigh Anne glowed. "She's finally found her one true love," friends remarked.

Collins knew Leigh Anne loved Michael when she started packing snacks for him. In just two weeks she learned all of Michael's favorite foods. Collins and Michael were on the Briarcrest track team together—Collins pole-vaulted, while Michael threw discus and shot put—and when they set off on a long road trip by bus, Leigh Anne made them sack lunches for the ride. She would hand Collins one bag and then hand her three more. "Here, these are for Michael." She packed all of his favorites: Doritos, ham sandwiches with mustard only, white powdered donuts, and Little Debbie Oatmeal Creme Pies. As an afterthought, she also tossed in peanut butter crackers and chocolate-covered raisins.

Michael said later, "She acted like she cared. Like she wanted to do for me and wanted to give. I never had that."

❦

Among other things, Leigh Anne discovered that Michael had never experienced the most fundamental kind of child care: he had never been to a doctor or had his vaccinations. She took him to our pediatrician, who announced that he needed thirteen shots. Michael hated the shots and he stopped talking to Leigh Anne for three days. The following year, when she insisted he go back for his annual flu shot, he glared. "You white people are obsessed with those shots," he said.

But Leigh Anne realized that she needed to catch up on fifteen years of unmet needs. One by one, she dealt with his most urgent issues, the basics of survival. After taking him to a doctor, it was, "Hey, this kid's never been to the dentist. We'd better get him in to see one."

As the weeks went by, it began to seem silly and inconvenient for us to take him to someone else's house or ferry him all the way out to Quinterio's. Half the time when he came to our house he wouldn't have his clothes because he had left them somewhere else.

One night after basketball practice Michael said he wanted to go to Quinterio's, so Sean wearily made the long drive down into Mississippi. They stopped at Sonic so Michael could place his usual order—three No. 2s with extra mustard— and then Sean dropped him at the trailer. By now it was almost nine o'clock, and as Sean turned around to make the drive home, he tried a shortcut. The Mississippi countryside was very dark, and he got lost. He drove around on the back roads until he had no idea where he was.

Sean pulled over, rolled down his window, and took a look around, hoping to see a street sign in the pitch dark. After a moment of peering helplessly into the blackness, Sean hit the button to roll the window back up—and heard a menacing growl. Out of the dark, a snarling German shepherd came hurtling at him. The dog lunged and Sean pounded on the button. It was a race between dog and window, and the dog hit the glass just as the window closed. Shaken, Sean put the car in gear and sprayed gravel as he accelerated out of there. Too unnerved to pull over again, he followed the road until it dead-ended in Holly Springs, Mississippi, forty full miles from Memphis.

This is stupid, Sean thought. *Why are we doing this?*

When Sean got home, we talked it over and decided to invite Michael to move in with us full-time. For weeks he had come and gone as he pleased, and each time he didn't spend the night, we worried.

Leigh Anne said, "He likes staying here, we like him staying here, and I think he wants to stay here." It was no great epiphany.

In a brief family meeting, we made sure Collins and S.J. would be okay with it. "Totally open to it," S.J said. Michael spent most of his time in S.J.'s playroom anyway, so it wouldn't mean much of a change.

When Leigh Anne asked Michael if he wanted to move in, he looked pleased and said shyly, "I don't think I want to leave."

Leigh Anne offered to drive Michael to Quinterio's to pick up his clothes. They consisted of two pairs of pants, three shirts, and a pair of shoes. Next they drove around to all of the other temporary quarters where he had left other belongings and odds and ends, which he stuffed in a large garbage bag.

Leigh Anne went out and bought him a dresser and a bed. Sean advised her to make it an oversized futon. There was a loft above S.J.'s bedroom that S.J. used as his upstairs playroom; we converted it to a bedroom.

And with that, Michael officially became a member of our household.

❦

Michael hardly had time to react to his new surroundings. We moved at such a hectic pace that he just did what we did. "This is what we do," Leigh Anne would say, and he would follow. He got up on Sundays and went to church with us, then came home and watched ball games on TV. We didn't know if he just went along with things because he didn't want to upset anyone or if he really enjoyed living this way.

It was only later that we understood how much he wanted inclusion, to be involved in our lives and routines. "Everybody around me was smart and had everything I wanted and needed," he said. "I just wanted to be a part of it."

It was a testament to Michael's fortitude and intelligence that he could absorb so much so fast. To S.J., Michael seemed to have a near-genius ability to teach himself things. Like long division. He lacked the basics in math, having missed so much school, yet he learned in three weeks what should have taken him three months. He showed a bent for creative writing and, somehow, in his travels through eleven public schools, he had also acquired lovely penmanship. He wrote beautiful cursive script. S.J.'s penmanship was awful; he envied Michael's.

Michael could teach himself to do just about anything—even when it frightened him. We belonged to Chickasaw Country Club, and when we took the kids to go swimming, he just jumped in the pool, even though he'd never had a formal lesson. He sank to the bottom and pushed himself back up, sank to the bottom and pushed himself back up. Gradually he taught himself how to make his way through water.

"That is *not* swimming," said Collins, the freestyle sprint champ. She taught him the strokes.

There were times when we worried that he was overwhelmed. He didn't know what he didn't know—and he didn't know when what he didn't know might embarrass him in public. When we went to an Italian restaurant and ordered a plate of calamari he was horrified and didn't want to eat it.

Fettuccine Alfredo made him tense. "Just try it," we'd say. Restaurant menus made him nervous; he was unfamiliar with so many of the items.

"Same as if you or me went to his place, we'd be nervous and quiet," S.J. pointed out.

As Collins, S.J., and Michael bonded, they swapped cultural references and caught up on the things they hadn't been exposed to. Michael didn't know Chanel, Collins had never heard of Lil Wayne. Once, when Collins was slicing up some cheese and crackers for a snack, Michael asked, "What kind of cheese is that?"

"It's cheddar."

He said, "It looks like that government cheese."

"What is that?"

"It's this nasty stuff the government gives you."

Michael explained that it was a long chunk of USDA-issued cheese that was meant to help needy families on food stamps stretch their meals. You found it at soup kitchens or food banks. He told Collins, "Oh, it's bad. It's supposed to last for a long time." He held out his hands like a yardstick.

Leigh Anne was determined to demystify white, upper-middle-class Memphis for Michael. She wanted him to be at ease, to belong, to know that he wasn't out of place. Whatever he might feel about River Oaks, whether he ultimately decided to take it or leave it, she wanted it to be *his* choice. It didn't matter where he was from or where he had been or what his past was. "I don't care whether he has a mother or a father," she said. "I just want him to be as comfortable as my other two children."

Leigh Anne undertook Michael's cultural instruction

with the same ruthless efficiency she had brought to his vaccinations and dental work. As our friend Michael Lewis explained, "A lot of people mistook knowingness for intelligence. He had been denied the life experiences that led to knowingness." Leigh Anne would make sure Michael *knew* the same things that white Memphis kids knew. She explained golf to him: eagles, birdies, pars, and bogies. When we took a road trip to see a Briarcrest game and stayed in a nice hotel, she explained the concierge floor: the appetizers and breakfast were free. We didn't have to hide food and take it back to our rooms; we could come and go and help ourselves as we wished.

Sometimes, we'd take Michael and various other kids out to eat in a group, so Leigh Anne could explain things to them together, and that way no one would feel inferior to the others, or inadequate. After several meals in fine dining establishments, we realized why kids who had not eaten out much preferred a TGI Friday's or an Applebee's: they could order from the pictures and be sure to get what they wanted. At more upscale restaurants, Leigh Anne ordered several different entrées and she would explain them one by one: this is veal picatta, this is marsala. She discussed food groups, sauces, and what utensils to use when a certain food was served.

Little by little, Leigh Anne broke down barriers and led Michael across them. She was his tour guide, and he followed dutifully, soaking up information. She took over his wardrobe. "Here," she'd say, and hand him an oxford cloth buttondown shirt. "Put this on."

On one occasion, Michael needed a new backpack. He was still in the habit of carrying his entire locker around with him because he had never known where he would be spending the night, and his backpacks were constantly ripping. Leigh Anne went out and bought him the strongest one she could find, a North Face. At first he seemed pleased and he loaded it up and took it off to school. But the next day he asked where his old one was.

"Out in the garbage," Leigh Anne said. "It was ripped."

Michael walked out the back door, headed toward the driveway to retrieve it.

"What are you doing?" Leigh Anne asked.

"The guys made fun of me today for having a North Face backpack. They said, 'Only rich kids carry those.'"

Leigh Anne sat Michael down on the couch and looked him in the eye. "Michael, you *are* rich now," she told him. "Tomorrow you look those smart alecks right in the face and say, 'You like my new backpack?' And then you go, 'Oh, by the way, I *am* a rich kid now.'"

He never mentioned the old backpack again.

❦

Left alone without Leigh Anne's prodding, Michael could lapse into a cavernous silence. He was hard to read and intensely private about his life before he met us. He had no discernible rage about his childhood and, as far as we could tell, few memories that he wanted to discuss. "He's not mad at anybody," Sean noticed. "He should be but he's not." He seemed to have channeled all of his emotions into ambition. As Sean put it, "He has a lot of fire but no anger."

We decided that it was a psychological mechanism: Michael didn't want to think about what had happened seven days ago, much less seven years ago. He just wanted to move forward. He didn't want to live in the past, and no doubt that's what saved him.

We agreed with his strategy—up to a point. We didn't want to dwell on the past, either; we were too busy helping him move forward, tending to his immediate needs, getting him situated in the house, and a dozen other things. But there was one aspect of his old life we felt he had to deal with. We encouraged him to visit his biological family. We didn't want our family to be a reason for Michael not having a relationship with them, and we wanted him to know that it was okay with us if he wanted to include them in whatever he did.

On occasion Michael liked to go back to his old neighborhood to get his hair cut at his favorite barbershop, and Collins would drive him downtown and pick him up afterward. She got an eyeful of the world he'd grown up in. It was such a derelict and dangerously gang-controlled area that most taxis refused to pass through.

Since Michael didn't like to talk much about his childhood, almost everything we knew about his past we learned from other people—from social workers and later from the research of our friend Michael Lewis. We learned that there was a time when he had lived in a car. We learned that he'd sometimes had to drink water just to get a full feeling in his stomach. We learned that he had an older brother named Marcus, who had done his best to care for his little brother when he was just a boy himself. It was a testament to Michael's willpower and survival skills that he had escaped that neighborhood without a police record or a bullet in him.

One day Michael announced out of the blue that he wanted

his license—no one in his family had ever had one. Plus, he was tired of having to rely on Collins for a ride.

Leigh Anne looked at Sean and said, "Do you think he knows how to drive?" We never knew what he did or didn't know, and we didn't want to expose or embarrass him.

"I don't know," Sean said. "Take him out in the car and find out."

Sure enough, he knew how to drive.

Michael beamed when he got his license. He passed the road test in Sean's 745 BMW.

※

There was no question, however, that Michael experienced strains, including some we weren't aware of. The problem was, he wouldn't tell us about them. When we saw that something was bothering him, we could only guess what it was. At one point, we suggested he talk to a therapist, but he didn't feel the need to.

Sometimes when he was worried or upset, Michael would leave and simply not come back for a couple of days. We didn't have any claim on him and he was free to come and go. Still, we would get anxious—and that's how we knew we were becoming his parents. To wait up for a child who's late coming home is a universal parental dread, and we began to experience it with Michael. No matter how watchful or careful we were, some small, seemingly innocuous thing would happen, and he would be gone. When he showed up again, we implored him to talk.

"If something bothers you, just tell us," Sean said.

It happened only a handful of times and a pattern emerged:

he'd almost always get restless when something was looming that he was feeling pressured by, like a test or a paper. When he came back, we'd say, "Next time tell us what's coming up, so we can help you *prepare* for it."

Eventually we learned that he always showed up at school. He'd return to Briarcrest and make his class on time, and he'd be punctual about getting to basketball or football practice. But he wouldn't say a word about what was bothering him. Sean would plead, "Michael. Just talk to us. If there's an issue, let's work it out."

Where did he go? We didn't ask. We guessed that when he was in crisis he went to sleep on a classmate's sofa, or to Quinterio's way down in Mississippi. We never did quite figure it out.

We'd say, "Michael, it's not fair to worry us like this. Tell us what's up."

"Yeah, okay."

And eventually, he did.

It was Leigh Anne who finally broke through and earned Michael's emotional trust. Or rather, seized it. At every turn she confronted him. She would say exactly what was on her mind—and she demanded that he say what was on his mind, too.

Every evening Leigh Anne would go into our kids' rooms and kiss them and tell them good night. A month or so after Michael first moved into the house, Leigh Anne went into his room, too.

She kissed him and said, "Good night, I love you."

There was no reply.

Nevertheless, Leigh Anne did it again the next night. And

the next. And the next. And every night afterward. For months, she went into his room and cheerfully gave him her love, without asking for it in return.

Finally, one night, Michael's voice floated out of the dark, like a pretty note from a cello string.

"I love you, too," he said.

✤

The single most fictional portrayal in *The Blind Side* didn't concern the cut of Leigh Anne's skirt—it was the idea that Michael Oher didn't know how to play football. We're big fans of John Lee Hancock, the movie's director, but it was pure cinematic nonsense when he had Leigh Anne (wearing spike heels, of course) show Michael how to block and then had an eight-year-old S.J. explain the playbook using salt-shakers.

In fact, by the time he got to us, Michael was already a fairly impressive athlete; all he lacked was polish. An educated eye like Sean's could see how agile he was—how he naturally loaded his hips and how lightly he bobbed on the balls of his feet. He was very strong, with arms the size of boa constrictors, and as he began losing some weight he quickly got into better shape. And he was fast: despite his size, he ran the forty-meter dash in just 4.9 seconds.

That said, none of us saw him as a future NFL superstar. At first, Sean thought he would be a better basketball player because he was so dexterous. It turned out that Michael was well known on the city's basketball courts, but he had spent only one unimpressive season on the football field for Westwood High as a defensive lineman. Sean's goal wasn't to groom Michael to play football at Ole Miss, much less the NFL. The goal was to help him to get a high school diploma, and Sean also thought that with some sound coaching, Michael could win a Division II scholarship—to play basketball.

Then the goal changed. In the fall of Michael's junior year, he blossomed. He was no longer overwhelmed by all he didn't know and he was now secure at home with us and confident in his ability to negotiate Briarcrest. His new self-assurance really began to show on the football field—physically, mentally, and emotionally.

Within weeks, he began picking up the finer points of playing left tackle. It was a difficult position to master. Offensive linemen are invariably some of the smartest guys on the team: line play is complex, with a lot of moving pieces and coordinated movements, and to play the position well you have to know everybody else's job as well as your own. But Michael learned how to play left tackle the way he learned everything: fast.

Michael had the benefit of some first-rate coaching. Briarcrest's head coach, Hugh Freeze, regularly took his teams to state championships in a variety of sports, including girls' basketball, and he had a gift for strategy that would shortly carry him to the college ranks. Sean always said of Hugh, "As long as you don't have more players than he does, he'll beat you."

Moreover, a couple of capable volunteer assistants on Hugh's staff were especially helpful to Michael. One was Tim Long, a six-foot-six former lineman who played college football at Memphis and spent two years in the NFL. The other was Sean.

Hugh had recently invited Sean to join the staff, primarily as a motivator because he was so good at building relationships with kids. When Hugh assigned Sean to the tight ends, Sean said, "I don't know anything about tight ends." Hugh said, "It's one guy, how hard can it be?"

The first time Sean came to practice, he drove up in his BMW. All the other coaches stared at it disapprovingly. A luxury car was . . . unmanly. "You can't coach in that," Hugh told him. The next day, Sean went out and bought a Ford pickup. He'd never had one before and he discovered that he didn't want to get out of it. (He's now on his third.)

Sean's relationship with Michael was very different than Leigh Anne's—it was no less emotional but it was more pragmatic. Partly that was because Michael refused to grant Sean the same intimacy he shared with Leigh Anne. He was happy to talk football and basketball with Sean, because that was their common ground. But beyond that Michael remained guarded.

"He just talks to me until you get home," Sean told Leigh Anne. "I'm the player to be named later."

Leigh Anne teased him back by saying, "You're just the ATM machine."

Michael's reserve drove Sean crazy, until he finally figured out that it wasn't about him. Michael didn't dislike him; he just didn't trust men. Which made perfect sense, since Michael had never had a father figure. Once Sean understood this, he decided that he was fine with their relationship exactly as it was. He loved Michael and although he wished Michael would come to him to talk about his feelings, that simply wasn't going to happen.

Instead, Sean became a mentor to Michael. He taught him how to play cards, spades and gin. He talked money matters with him, went over the playbook with him, and managed his competitive crises. Collins, for one, began to notice a trend. When it came to personal things, Michael went to either her or Leigh Anne. But if he encountered a more practical problem, Michael went straight to Sean.

❦

As Michael's junior season of playing football for Briarcrest went on, Sean became more involved in teaching him the subtler aspects of the game. At home, Sean used Leigh Anne's dining chairs to map out the field action for Michael. He even used the dining table to form the defensive line—when Leigh Anne was out of the house.

Michael steadily improved and soon he was flattening opponents like a lawn mower cuts grass. You could see the physics beginning to kick in. Football is about moving heavy things, physically repositioning the opponent. In Michael's case, movement was exclusively *his* choice. When he surged off the line, it was like watching a huge wave hit the defense. But if you wanted to move him, good luck. It was easier to dislodge a wall.

By the end of that fall Michael had a pretty impressive highlights reel. One day, Sean talked to Tim Long about Michael's developing ability as a football player. "Do you think he could get a football scholarship?" he asked Tim.

"You know," Tim said, "Someone's going to take him."

Late that fall, Sean's old classmate Michael Lewis came to

visit. They had known each other since kindergarten and played baseball together at Newman, but they hadn't seen each other in years. Lewis was writing an article for the *New York Times Magazine* about their old coach Billy Fitzgerald and arrived in Memphis to interview Sean for the piece. After a couple of evenings of talking over Newman glories, Lewis finally asked the question that had been nagging at him.

"I'm sorry," he said, "but who *is* that large black kid sitting at your dining table?"

"Well," Sean said, "that young man is living here, and he's become like a son to us. We're talking about adopting him."

Sean explained what little we knew about Michael's circumstances and told Lewis how far he'd come in the classroom and how much promise he showed as an athlete.

Fascinated, Lewis went home and told his wife, Tabitha, all about the meeting. Her response was to ask: "Why are you writing about anything else?"

Lewis called us back and asked if we'd mind if he did a piece about Michael for the *Times*. Sean and Michael talked it over. "You've worked so hard," Sean said. "It might be good for you and it might help you get noticed by some coaches at the bigger schools." We all agreed to give Lewis the go-ahead.

So that's how Lewis came to author the book entitled *The Blind Side*, which was excerpted in the *New York Times Magazine* in a piece called "The Ballad of Big Mike."

This is the point at which Michael always chimes in, whenever we tell the story:

"And then I became an all-American," he says.

One evening in the spring of Michael's junior year, Hugh Freeze called us at home with some astonishing news. *USA Today* was naming Michael the No. 1 recruit in America.

Sean said, "Are you talking about basketball?"

No, said Hugh, and then he explained that a renowned football scout named Tom Lemming had watched film of Michael and identified him as one of the best high school offensive linemen he'd ever seen. Suddenly, it seemed, we had the most sought-after football player in the country living in an upstairs bedroom.

"I don't get it," Sean said to Hugh.

"His last couple games he really started coming on," Hugh said. "And he's just so talented."

But the biggest event for all of us that spring was our adoption of Michael. Actually, this was just a formality, the legal completion of an emotional process that had started long before. In our hearts and our minds, Michael was now our third child. We'd already put him on our insurance policies, added him to the trust funds, and written him into our will. In December 2004, we included him in our family Christmas card picture with S.J. and Collins for the first time.

To tell the truth, Leigh Anne considered Michael a lot more cooperative than our other kids in some ways. "I personally think I birthed Michael," Leigh Anne would say. "I know he doesn't look like it."

Or she would point first at Collins and then at Michael and teasingly say, "I got stuck with her. I *picked* him."

So the idea of adopting Michael came to us quite naturally. One evening we told him that we wanted to formally become his guardians. It wasn't an executive family session or anything. We were all just lounging around the dining table.

"We're thinking of making this official," Leigh Anne told him. "How do you feel about that?"

We explained that it would require some paperwork. We told him that his biological mother would have to appear in court to give her consent, but that we felt adopting him would be a good idea.

That's when he said, "I already thought I was part of the family."

We said, "You are."

"Well, let's go do it then."

"Okay, fine," Leigh Anne said.

We knew that people would talk when they found out we had adopted Michael. But we were also pretty sure that no one would ever have the guts to say anything to our faces. "And if they did, I would tell them, 'Don't let the door hit your butt on the way out,'" Leigh Anne said.

But a number of people did talk to Leigh Anne about a different issue. In hushed, self-conscious tones, they would ask, "How do you handle it?"

She knew what they meant: these folks had a hang-up because we had brought a black, teenaged male into the house with a daughter the same age. The implication was clear: a black kid couldn't control his libido. We got some nasty letters and came across some ugly innuendos on the Internet. But very quickly we realized that we'd go crazy if we worried about every little comment sent our way.

Sometimes Sean would read something aloud—a letter, or a snide remark he saw on the Internet.

Leigh Anne would go into her hands-on-hips, woman-warrior mode and say, "I want to find out where they live!"

She lost her Internet privileges for a while.

What Leigh Anne really wanted to say to people was, "I'm looking in your windows right now and you could be doing a little housekeeping of your own. So don't you be sitting there worrying about what's going on under *my* roof when *you've* got kids who are out smoking dope, having sex, and whatever."

What she actually said was more polite. When someone would subtly question her judgment, she would just say, "You need to mind your own business. You worry about your own life and I'll worry about mine."

After all: who owns the blueprint on the best way to raise a child? Nobody.

❦

We were, however, well aware of a legitimate debate about race in adoption. Some advocates even wanted to forbid "transracial placement," to use the chilly government phrase for it. A lot of strong language got thrown around: opponents, for instance, argued that whites could rob a child of his or her "cultural identity."

Did we rob Michael of his identity? The simple truth is, all we ever wanted to do was help him achieve an identity. We can only contribute our own personal observation to the discussion: it never seemed to bother Michael that his adoptive parents were of a different race. All that mattered was that he had love and opportunity that he might not have had otherwise.

"I don't understand why people would feel that way," Michael said years later. "As long as somebody is helping somebody and taking them off the streets, I don't care—you know, black or white or whatever, it should never be a problem."

Did race come up? You bet. At a basketball tournament in Myrtle Beach, South Carolina, a bunch of rednecks called him the n-word. Michael responded by giving them the middle finger, which Leigh Anne heartily approved of. And sometimes an opposing team's fans would chant at him, "Tu-ohy's Mon-ey!"

When Briarcrest held a prom, we wanted to rent a tuxedo for Michael at a local shop. Just before Leigh Anne set off on her daily power walk, she said, "Michael, go down to the rental place and look around—see what you like. I'll come down after my workout and we'll pick out a tux together."

A little while later, Michael came back to the house and called her on her cell phone. "They didn't want me to look because I didn't have any money," he told her.

Leigh Anne said grimly, "I'll be there in just a minute."

She didn't make a huge issue out of it; she just marched into the establishment and said, "This is my *son*. We'd like to see what you have in a fifty-eight-inch chest."

To be honest, we seldom thought about race in regard to Michael because we were too busy just trying to parent him. We had too many other, more urgent matters. But Harvard Law professor Randall Kennedy, author of *Interracial Intimacies: Sex, Marriage Identity and Adoption*, summed up our feelings best. "Parenting is a mysterious thing," Kennedy has said. "People will learn what they need to learn in order to help their child along. I'm willing to assume that with respect to all parents, including white people who adopt black kids."

As for people who wanted to focus on the "rich white family saves poor black athlete" angle, they profoundly oversimplified a complicated story, which did no good for anyone who wanted to understand how Michael wound up in his situation and how he worked his way out of it.

Plenty of black families offered Michael a hand before he met us, particularly the Franklins. And plenty of both black and white people in Memphis failed Michael miserably. Public schools allowed him to reach his teenaged years with a very low reading level, and child services lost track of him entirely.

So, yes, race was a factor in his life, but much more important was Michael's self-determination. That was a neutral quality; it had nothing to do with color. A black family could have adopted him, or he could have been a 120-pound flute player. Whatever, the outcome would have been just the same: Michael was *going* to succeed. And if we had a bottom line in this debate, it was this: as a community, *all* of us had to give more to *all* children in similar circumstances.

As a family, we couldn't afford to be thin-skinned. If we listened to the naysayers and the critics and the gossips, it would ruin our lives. We resigned ourselves to it: Michael would get ridiculed for living with a white family, and Collins and S. J. would be ridiculed for having a black brother. But we simply couldn't worry about what everybody else thought.

"All that matters is the five of us," Leigh Anne told the kids. "What matters is that *the five of us know where our hearts are.*"

✤

Our joy trumped all other feelings or considerations: it was wonderful to have another child in the house. It's no exaggeration to say that Michael brought all of us closer. Because of him we spent a lot more time together around the dining table, which was a long rectangular affair in an open communal area between the kitchen and the den. Before Michael, we were always on the go, always on different schedules. Collins would have cheerleading practice until seven thirty, but S.J. would be hungry at six. Or Sean would be traveling, while Leigh Anne was off somewhere on a project. We all did our own thing, and came and went on our own time lines.

But when Michael moved in, everyone somehow got on the same page. The table became our hub. Michael and Collins got out of practice at the same time in the evening and they would come home and sit down to study together at the table. When they broke for dinner, the rest of us naturally began to join them. S.J. would wander over, so Sean would sit down to have a bite and chat. Then Leigh Anne would drift by, making sure everyone had what they needed. Michael was like a centrifugal force that pulled us all together. Sometime between six and nine every night we were always at the table, talking, studying, eating, or laughing.

Somehow, our kids came together like the perfect storm. One thing we were utterly confident in was the relationship among the three of them. We never had to worry about whether they got along—they did. Nor did we worry that Collins or S.J. would resent Michael for taking us away from them—they didn't.

In fact, Collins confessed later that having Michael around gave her a respite from our focus. "I don't ever remember feeling I had to fight for anyone's attention," she said. "Honestly, if anything I felt a little relieved that some attention was taken off me." It was a quiet joke among the kids that the intensity of our concern for Michael actually took some heat off Collins and S.J.

That's not to say the three of them didn't fight—but they fought like brothers and sister. S.J and Michael shared the upper story of the house and they were perpetually tethered together to the video console, over which they sometimes bickered. If anyone should have minded Michael's adoption it was S.J., who had to cede some of his territory to him and share a bathroom. Until Michael arrived, S.J. had always ruled the upstairs den alone, so we waited for him to object, to say, "Maybe this adoption thing isn't such a good idea, guys. I mean, it was fine at first but now he's moving into my room."

But S.J. was all for it, because it meant he'd have full access to Michael for their epic, never-ending Xbox game, as well as a built-in big brother to look after him. Besides, S.J. was precocious; he had been raised with a sister who was seven years older than he was. To him, getting a big brother was a fabulous development—he got access to all of Michael's practices and unlimited rides to wherever he wanted to go.

Michael looked after S.J. when we went out of town to cheerleading meets with Collins. He got him up for school, fed him, and drove him around town. They spent hours in the driveway playing basketball, horsing around with fade-aways and crossover dribbles. Michael lowered the ten-foot hoop so S.J. could dunk. To even up the mismatch in games of one-on-one, S.J. declared that Michael couldn't play in the post, he could only shoot from the outside. In the evenings, Michael made S.J. watch the BET show *106 & Park*—which got S.J. rapping. S.J. also learned most of the dialogue in *Boyz N the Hood*, though he didn't dare quote it around us.

If anything, Collins was even closer to Michael. They were track teammates, they shared a lot of the same classes at school, and they became confidants in a way that wasn't possible with S.J. because he was so much younger. They were proud of each other and looked after each other. Collins was a cheerleader on the sidelines of every football game, and at halftime Michael would stick his head out of the locker room door to watch her perform. And Collins was always bringing Michael things he had forgotten at home—like his helmet.

Whenever guys would try to flirt with Collins, Michael would amble over and loom above their heads.

"I see you're talking to my sister."

"No, no, we were just saying hey," they'd say, and flee.

By now, Collins had supplanted Leigh Anne as Michael's fashion consultant. Once he became a heavily recruited athlete, Michael had to entertain visits from football coaches and so dress like a collegian. Collins supervised his wardrobe for these encounters.

On the day that coach Phillip Fulmer of Tennessee came to visit, Collins was appalled by Michael's selection of clothes. "You *cannot* wear black pants to go with a blue blazer." When Michael tried to shrug her off, Collins stole his pants and ran out of the room with them.

Michael chased her down the stairs, wearing nothing but his underwear. Squealing and giggling, Collins dashed into the living room, while Michael, right on her heels, thundered, "Give me back my pants!"

Sitting uncomfortably in the pointless living room was Coach Fulmer.

Michael, bare-legged, ignored him. He grabbed Collins,

snatched back his black pants, and threw both his pants and his sister over his shoulder. Then he turned and marched out of the living room.

As Michael carried her upstairs, Collins called to Coach Fulmer: "Tell him they don't match!"

But at least on that day, Michael couldn't win—Collins stole the pants back and hid them. Finally, he was forced to put on a navy pair.

Once Michael had dressed and left the house with Coach Fulmer—who ended up becoming a friend of the family—Collins and a friend took out Michael's enormous, fifty-inch-waist black britches. Collins stepped in one leg and her friend stepped in the other. Then they got our friend Miss Sue Mitchell to take a photograph, and later Collins was delighted to give the photo to Michael as a souvenir of her victory.

❦

Ours was a tumultuous household, to say the least. In addition to three large and antic children, we also had a cat—and then we acquired three goldfish. S.J. won them at a fair and proudly brought them home in a large clear plastic bag, leaving Leigh Anne no alternative but to buy an aquarium for them. She put the aquarium in the kitchen under a light, where the fish prospered.

One of the fish grew so big he became twice as big as the others. One morning Leigh Anne stared at the three fish through the glass and said, "They're sort of like Michael, Collins, and S.J."

It became part of Leigh Anne's morning routine to feed the fish. She would pad into the kitchen for her morning Diet

Coke and, while she waited for the fizz to go down, she would flip on the light above the fish tank and shake some food into it. The goldfish brought out a major contradiction in Leigh Anne—her dual feistiness and sensitivity. Each time she flicked on the light to feed the goldfish, they would splash around in apparent excitement, and she started imagining that the splashing meant they were glad to see her. She thought she had a *relationship* with the fish.

But then tragedy struck, as so often happens with twenty-five-cent goldfish. Leigh Anne went out of town with Collins to a cheerleading competition, leaving the boys at home. The next morning, Michael came into the kitchen to find that one of the fish had died. It came as no surprise, really; he was a cheap little fish, bred in a carnival and spawned in a cloudy tank of water.

But Michael knew how upset Leigh Anne would be. First, he got a net and dipped the little fish corpse out of the tank. Next, he flushed it down a toilet so Leigh Anne wouldn't have to see it. Finally, he decided he had to break the news to her himself.

He called Leigh Anne on her cell phone and said, "Listen, we had a problem." Gently he told her that one of the fish had died. "But don't worry," he said, "I've taken care of it."

Leigh Anne immediately burst into tears. She cried and cried over the loss.

Trying to comfort her, Michael told her, "The worst part was, he was floating on his back."

Leigh Anne wailed at the image.

The other two fish survived just a few more months

before they too passed away. "I think they died of loneliness," Leigh Anne said mournfully.

The life and death of goldfish won at a children's fair is part of a time-honored family ritual. The purchase of a fish tank, the lecture to a solemn-eyed child about caring for a pet, the ritual of shaking the fish food over the water's surface— these are the passages, devotions, and daily transitions that make family life. And Michael was now an inextricable part of our family. He came downstairs one morning, stood in our kitchen, and dealt with the dead goldfish. As far as we were concerned, that was as strong a bond as any legal document.

As a family, we had a powerful sense that we were meant to be together. The way we looked at it, we'd been given the gift of another child and we were smart enough not to turn our backs.

Why? We believe faith played a part in it. Michael could have been in thirteen different classes, but he happened to be in our daughter's. He could have attended thirteen different private schools, but he went to ours. He could have been walking down another street that day before Thanksgiving, but he walked down ours. He could have been much less receptive to us, but instead he opened his heart.

So when even the most well-meaning people sometimes treat Michael as different, as separate from our other children, we take great offense. More often than we care to admit, people suggest that we have only two real kids. They'll say, "You have two children and Michael."

Leigh Anne will reply, "No, I have *three* children. And if you say that again, they're gonna be fighting words."

Once, when we were young expectant parents, our pediatrician tried to explain childbirth to us. He finally said, "We could talk about why it works for the next six hours. Or you could just accept that it's a miracle."

We feel the same way about Michael.

INTERLUDE

Michael Oher

SON

IMAGINE A SEVEN-YEAR-OLD KID, ALL ALONE AND MILES away from home. Imagine him making it by himself to the other side of town, where he stands in front of stores, looking in the windows for something to eat. I was in that situation a thousand times. I wouldn't have a place to stay. I'd sleep in a car one night and I'd sleep on a porch the next night. I was just trying to survive another night.

But I've always had a strong will. I knew at thirteen years old I was going to be something. Whether I was an athlete, a basketball or football player, or a nonathlete, I was going to have a successful life. Coming across the Tuohys made my road so much easier but, even if I hadn't run across them, I was still going to be something. It would've been a lot harder—but I was going to do it.

I grew up very tough, homeless, not eating a lot. I went to school just to eat. I came from a neighborhood where nobody makes it out. Zero make it out. There was a lot of violence, a lot of drugs, and a lot of bad people. But there's a reason I didn't go in that direction: I wasn't going to get off course. I wasn't going to get caught up in the ghetto. I was going to get out. I was going to go to work and do something. One thing I've always done was stay true to myself.

People ask me, how did I survive? You just wait, and keep your head up. I just kept going, knowing it had to get better. It can't get any worse than the situation that I was in. So, if you're going through any kind of problem, I can tell you: it's going to get better. It has no choice. If you just stay focused and keep doing the right thing, it has no choice but to get better.

The Lord kept his hand on me by finding the Tuohy family, my family, and bringing me to them. That was nothing but the man above. I was blessed to be taken in by a family that showed me a lot, taught me a lot. It was one of the best feelings I ever had. I just needed that chance. It's interesting because other people had the opportunity to help me, Sean and Leigh Anne weren't the only ones who knew my situation. But they were the two who stepped in and reached out.

It wasn't important to them where I was from, and I still can't believe that. To take somebody from my neighborhood into your house? Nobody does that. I don't think I'd even do that. With all the violence and drugs where I come from? They've got big hearts.

I always felt part of their family. It was never an awkward feeling. They opened their hearts to me and it's like we've been together from day one. I was going from house to house, but at other people's houses I'd get the feeling they didn't want me there. With the Tuohys, it was like I belonged there, and they wanted me there. They all welcomed me with open arms. I felt like, there was my mom, there was my dad, and there was my little brother S.J., and my sister Collins. And we went from there.

Looking back on it, I probably would have been jealous or upset if somebody was moving in my house and taking all my parents' time. But nobody got mad, nobody got upset because I got attention, there wasn't any of that. They just took me in like I was a big brother. I'm pretty sure they get it from their mom and dad rubbing off on them. That's just the way they were raised.

We spent most of our time at the dining table. Everybody would be at that table and we grew so close around it. We'd eat, study; we bonded around it, and revolved around it. It was where we always were, where everything happened.

I don't dwell on the past. I'm not going to feel sorry for myself because I didn't have a place to stay a lot of the time. It is what it is. Take it and run with it. That's why I'll never, ever wake up one day and be comfortable with my situation—it'll always be unbelievable. But I am never ashamed of where I came from. I think it has made me a better player, a tougher person.

5

Giving and Getting

LEIGH ANNE and SEAN

We all need someone to have our back.

—LEIGH ANNE TUOHY

IT WAS AMAZING TO SEE HOW A YOUNG MAN CHANGED when he felt loved, full, and smart. One day Sean and S.J. walked into the house to find Michael sitting at the dining table before an elegant place setting of food. For an appetizer he had a plate of calamari, for his entrée, lobster fettuccine. He was drinking a Shirley Temple, and a linen napkin was folded over his knee as neatly as if he were the Prince of Wales at a picnic.

Sean stared at him and said, "Wow."

"What?"

"You're sitting there, eating calamari and lobster Alfredo. You have come a loooong way."

Michael just gazed back at him for a moment.

"I don't know what you're talking about," he said. "I'm just eating dinner."

The boy who was once so ill at ease had become a sophisticate. He had won command of subjects that it took our daughter a leisurely lifetime to learn. He had achieved "knowingness."

But Michael faced one last hurdle: in order to be academically eligible to play college football under NCAA rules, he would need to raise his grade point average. By the end of his junior year, he had become a solid student who was passing in every subject, but it wasn't enough. By Sean's calculations he would have to make all As and Bs as a senior—and, even then, he might not make it.

"It's going to be close," Sean said.

Sean had a suggestion: rather than put so much pressure on himself, Michael should consider delaying college. After his final year at Briarcrest, he could enroll in Hargrave Military Academy, a private school in Chatham, Virginia, where promising college athletes often spent an extra year after high school improving their grades.

"You can take your time and have a nice senior year like everyone else," Sean said. "It won't be hard. You just don't have enough time to get it all done."

But Michael was one of the top recruits in America. Pride crept into his voice when he said, "No. That would be a setback. I'm ready to go to college and get to work—I'm going for it."

If that was what Michael wanted, then we wanted it for him. We went into action. That night, "Team Oher" was formed at our dining table. We mapped out our strategy and put together a lineup of cheerful givers committed to giving Michael every chance of succeeding. Our first call was to our friend Sue Mitchell, a former Ole Miss Kappa Delta, who was part of Leigh Anne's sisterhood.

Sue had taught English in the Shelby County public school system for thirty-nine years. She was not only a thoroughly dedicated teacher, she was a driven competitor. She had led Bartlett High School's cheerleading squad to five national championships and her motto was "We win, or else." We knew that Sue, of all people, would fight with everything she had to help Michael reach his goals.

Michael's academic push became a communal project. Everybody jumped in and did something to help. Jill Freeze, the wife of Briarcrest's football coach, tutored Michael in math, as did Liz Marable. Our close friend and attorney Debbie Branan was always on hand to help him with Spanish vocabulary words. Sue Mitchell's colleague Jacque Higdon, a school librarian, would ferry books to the house anytime we needed sources for projects. Half a dozen wonderful people came and went with happy hearts, eager to give Michael a boost.

One evening, the executive board of Team Oher wound up in our bedroom. Sean and Leigh Anne were having a disagreement about whether Michael needed to take on an extra-credit project. Sean thought he was pulling too much of a load, while Leigh Anne thought the opposite, and they went into the bedroom to discuss it. After a few minutes, Sean yelled, "Sue, get in here." Sue came in to voice her opinion and Debbie followed her. Then Sue called out to Jacque, who had brought some books over, "Jacque, come on in here." Sean turned to her and said, "What do you think?"

Jacque said, "I'm Switzerland. I'm neutral."

Sean said, "That is not allowed. In this house you take a stand. And you never give up on it whether you're right or wrong."

The key to Michael's academic performance was not how smart he was, it was how organized he was. Leigh Anne called each of Michael's teachers at Briarcrest and asked them what he could do to pull his grades up. "Just give me the list," she said. If he could earn extra credit for reading a certain book, or doing a project, he would do it.

We were going to see that Michael had everything he needed to succeed, from the right books to the best compass. With Collins and S.J., Sean had seen what Leigh Anne's powers of organization could accomplish. She never seemed to have a moment of lazy parenting. While other kids in kindergarten were still trying to find Popsicle sticks for a project, Leigh Anne would have our kids' all laid out. If a middle school teacher announced on January 1 that a report was due on April 5, that thing was done on March 5. The last month was spent watching everyone else rush to finish.

Sean had never seen another mother who could make her kids do that. "You're phenomenal," Sean marveled. "I hate you for some of the things you do, but you're phenomenal."

He added, teasing, "I don't know if I could be your kid. But they seem to hang in there."

In Michael, we had the perfect teammate. Most kids his age would take four steps forward and two steps back. They inevitably slacked off. But Michael understood that if for every four steps he took, he never took a step back, he could double his progress. He figured out where he needed to go and the fastest method of getting there—and that was to do every single thing Leigh Anne told him to do.

Most students at Briarcrest had seven periods a day. That fall, Michael had eight. He'd arrive at school at six thirty for an hour of extra-credit work. Then he'd plow through seven hours of classes. After that, he'd go to football practice, come home and take a shower, and sit down to several more hours of study with Sue and every other tutor on his schedule. Six nights a week, he worked until at least eleven, and sometimes into the early hours of the morning.

One evening early in his senior year, he came home and dropped his backpack heavily. We thought we saw tears in his eyes.

"I can't do this," he said.

"I know it," Sean said, looking at him sympathetically. He was on Michael's side. It wasn't that Sean thought Michael couldn't do it—nobody could. *There ain't no way*, Sean thought. *I could never have done the stuff he's doing at his age.*

But then Leigh Anne's voice rang out.

"No," she said. "We're going to do it. You're going to sit your butt down, and we're going to do it. We don't give up on anything around here."

Michael reached for his backpack and took up his books again. The next morning on his way out the door to school, Leigh Anne told him, "Suck it up."

Collins helped support Michael throughout his academic marathon—and she gave up some things, too. Senior year in high school is a big deal for teenagers, and Collins was a candidate for homecoming queen. Even so, she rearranged her entire schedule. Though she was an honors student in several Advanced Placement classes, she dropped them to be in Michael's English and math classes instead, and spent hours studying with him at the dining table every night.

Michael and Collins were extremely close—which was not to say they didn't bicker. One afternoon they got into it about who was the faster runner: Collins was a good sprinter in the one hundred and two hundred meters, while Michael ran a very fast forty meters. They started jawing back and forth at each other, and pretty soon Collins was tying on her sneakers and saying, "Lace 'em up, Michael. Let's go outside right now." She was going to race him right on Shady Grove Lane.

Sean beamed; he was all for it. But Leigh Anne put her foot down. She could not tolerate the idea of them jeopardizing their athletic careers because they ruptured an Achilles tendon in a street race. "You are absolutely not going out there to do that," she said.

Collins sulked. "I could have taken him. It wouldn't have been close. I could have *smoked* him in the one hundred for sure." It became a standing family joke. Sean would say, "So, are ya'll gonna lace up this year?"

Watching Collins study with Michael was like watching one runner pace another. Collins took careful class notes every day so that Michael would have them if he needed them—she knew he wasn't a great note taker, though he could memorize anything. Sometimes Collins brought her friends over to make studying more enjoyable for him, and the dining table would fill up, especially before a test. Heaped in the midst of the table would be all the papers they were working with, laid out just the way they needed them—but then Leigh Anne would swoop in with the Windex bottle. She'd announce that there were too many fingerprints on the tabletop, and they'd all have to pick up their books so she could spray it.

There was no question Michael could do the work—the only question was whether he would run out of time. It frustrated him to go backward; he only wanted to go forward. English was at once his best and most difficult subject. He could recite whole passages of *Macbeth*, but he was impatient when Sue would want to review. She'd say, "Okay, let's go back." Michael didn't want to go back. He'd say, "I got it, Miss Sue, I got it."

When Miss Sue and Collins would take a break and watch *American Idol*, he got exasperated.

He'd say, "Ya'll need to quit that stuff. We need to get to work here."

It was a long, mentally exhausting grind. He tried to cram in so much so fast that sometimes he couldn't read another sentence. "We've done this for so long," he'd say. "I just can't do this anymore." He would get up from the table and walk out the door, but he'd only stay away an hour or so. He'd play some basketball to blow off steam, and Sue would wait patiently while he cleared his head. Then he'd come back and be ready to work again.

Michael's load never got lighter—he pulled a heavy sled the whole year. After football season came basketball, and he was Tennessee's runner-up for "Mr. Basketball." After basketball came track, and he broke the sectional record in the discus. How he was able to expend all that physical energy and still have the strength to study until late at night, we didn't know.

Sean marveled at it. He would clap Michael on the back and say to him, "How's it going, All-World?"

Occasionally, Michael's tutors would get a glimpse of the stress he was feeling. One day at practice, one of his teammates tore his knee ligaments, and the injury unnerved Michael. His whole future was riding on an athletic scholarship. What if he got hurt?

Later, Michael brought up the subject while talking with Liz. Would everybody feel the same way about him? Or did they just care about him because he was a good athlete?

"Man, what if I blew my knee out? What would happen?" he asked.

"Michael, if you blow your knee out, or if anything else happens to you, you'll always have a home and family with Sean and Leigh Anne," Liz said.

"Will I?"

"You'll see. They'll love you to eternity. I can tell you from personal experience, when they love you, it's not for a day, it's not for a reason, it's not for a season. They will love you forever."

❦

The fall of his senior year, Michael made a loving gesture in return, one that showed how much he appreciated the support he was getting. He never said a word—his own style of giving— but he quietly went to work on Collins's behalf when she ran for Briarcrest Homecoming Queen. Collins didn't talk about how much fun it would be to win, but Michael sensed how she felt during their hours of studying at the table. After all the cheering she'd done for the football team, he thought she deserved it. Michael lobbied his classmates and, on the day of the election, he opened the door to each of the homerooms, stuck his head in, and called out: "Vote for Collins for homecoming queen!" Later Collins heard from half the school what he had done.

It was a silly thing, but high school elections can be fraught and it meant everything to Collins that Michael supported her without being asked. From then on she knew he was in her corner, no matter what.

Collins asked Michael to escort her in the homecoming presentation at the pep rally. As we watched him usher her, we knew he'd come into his own. A year or two earlier we'd have been nervous for him. We'd have wondered, (a) is he going to be there on time? and (b) will he show up in the right clothes? But there he was wearing a blazer with slacks and a matching tie, and he looked dashing.

The big moment came, and when the MC announced, "Our senior homecoming queen is Collins Tuohy, escorted by her brother, Michael Oher!" Michael sailed Collins across the floor like he was a debonair Cary Grant and she was Grace Kelly. Five minutes later he appeared in the senior skit. He came out in a pair of black shades and danced to "Eye of the Tiger," with the whole school chanting, "Mike, Mike, Mike!"

When Michael's final report card came, he'd made all As and Bs. The guarded kid we first met had become a self-confident, outgoing young man. We liked to think he still needed us, but he really didn't. Now he was fully equipped. He even had his own ride, a black pickup truck that Sean bought for him.

On May 25, 2005, Michael and Collins received their diplomas. Everyone applauded all the graduates, but when Michael walked across the stage to get his degree the audience whistled with special appreciation, and Briarcrest's principal, Steve Simpson, burst into a huge sunbeam of a grin as he shook Michael's hand.

That night we all talked about what a long saga it had been. "I'm the first one out of anybody that I ever knew to graduate," Michael said. He was finally on the same page with everybody else.

※

But Michael still had some academic work to finish: there hadn't been enough hours in the day to satisfy NCAA academic requirements, and he had simply run out of time. But Sean found an independent study program offered by Brigham Young University, and if Michael took it over the summer he could qualify. So right after graduation, Michael went back to work.

A series of "character education" courses required Michael to read about courageous figures and study their values. These classes became another excuse for Team Oher to gather around the dinner table and for us to enjoy each other's company as a family. But they also showed us a road map for engaging a young mind: anyone looking to get involved with a kid through a big brother or after-school program could do worse than to feed the child's imagination by reading about these great characters.

A biography of Lou Gehrig captivated Michael. He was deeply affected by the story of the poor son of a drunk and a maid from Second Avenue in New York City who grew up to play for the Yankees only to be struck by a neurological disease. Michael couldn't get over the unfairness of it when Gehrig lost his strength and stumbled around the bases. He read about how Gehrig, weakened by illness, started to fall as he crossed a street in an ice storm—and four strangers reached out and gave him a hand. "You have to get knocked down to realize how people really feel about you," Gehrig said. Michael could relate. So could we all.

When he read "The Charge of the Light Brigade," Michael struggled to understand the motives of men who rode into a massacre. Sean leaped to his feet and acted it out—it was one of his favorite poems from boyhood.

> Half a league, half a league,
> Half a league onward,
> All in the valley of Death
> Rode the six hundred.
>
> Cannon to right of them,
> Cannon to left of them,
> Cannon in front of them
> Volley'd and thunder'd;
> Storm'd at with shot and shell,
> Boldly they rode and well,
> Into the jaws of Death,
> Into the mouth of Hell
> Rode the six hundred.

"Why would they do that?" Michael asked. Sean explained it in football terms. "It's the same as when it's fourth and eight," he said. "When the coach calls the play, you don't question the reason why he wants to do it. You may not think it's right. But it's not your choice. You just execute it, right?"

Sometimes Michael would go off and read something by himself, and then he'd come back to the table and we'd talk about it. Sometimes Sue read aloud to him. Sometimes he read aloud to her. But when he read *Pygmalion*, we all got involved. The entire family acted out George Bernard Shaw's play, struggling in our Memphis accents through the intricate dialogue and plot, the story of Professor Henry Higgins's wager that he could remake that "draggle-tailed guttersnipe" Eliza Doolittle. Michael was the young love interest, Freddy, and when he came across a cuss word in the script, he wouldn't say it.

We went around the table:

> Remember that you are a human being with a soul and the divine gift of articulate speech: that your native language is the language of Shakespeare and Milton and The Bible; and don't sit there crooning like a bilious pigeon.

Or:

> The great secret, Eliza, is not having bad manners or good manners or any other particular sort of manners, but having the same manner for all human souls: in short, behaving as if you were in Heaven, where there are no third-class carriages, and one soul is as good as another.

We couldn't have agreed with the sentiment more.

Once Michael finished the correspondence courses he had to report to an independent test site to take his exams. But he wasn't nervous—he was prepared and he hit the ball out of the park. Sean airmailed the package of grades and paperwork off to the appropriate departments. He would have hand carried it if need be, after all the work Michael had put in. The Evil Empire that governs college athletes finally sent word back (somewhat grudgingly, we sensed): Michael was eligible to play football.

The Brigham Young program was a valuable tool for us, though cynics would question our use of it. *Entertainment Weekly* even ran a piece entitled "Why *The Blind Side* Is Too Good to Be True," calling it an "eligibility trick." But Michael's epic struggle to get his grades up was an unbelievable act of will and determination, and nothing made us angrier than hearing people belittle his accomplishment. It would have been so easy, at any point, for Michael to give himself an out, or an excuse to fail, or to rebel. Instead, he did every single thing that was asked of him. The fact that he would go on to make the honor roll at Ole Miss would vindicate him and prove that there was nothing dubious about his classroom achievements. He put in the work and he deserved the credit.

Michael had chosen Ole Miss after a fair amount of recruiting drama, and a certain amount of flirtation with Tennessee, LSU, and Oklahoma State. Some people said we'd put the fix in for our alma mater. But how smart would it have been for Michael to pour so much work into preparing for college, only to go off to some place where he'd have considerably less support than he was used to?

At Ole Miss, he could stay close to us and continue to work with Sue. Sean offered to hire Sue full-time as Michael's private tutor and pay for her to move to Oxford, but Sue had a different opportunity. She had applied to Ole Miss for a position as a learning specialist in their academic support unit and been hired. Sue would still be able to work with Michael, but she would work with eight to ten other athletes as well.

Michael was no different from any other kid who didn't want to be too far away from his friends and family. "Ole Miss was right down the road," Michael said, "and I figured it would be easier for my family and my friends to get down to Oxford to come see me play."

✿

Frankly, Michael had more of a choice about where to go to college than Collins ever did. She was brainwashed where Ole Miss was concerned, and she was equally indoctrinated when it came to which sorority to pledge. Leigh Anne had fed Collins with a Kappa Delta baby bottle when she was an infant and she wasn't going to stand for a daughter who grew up to be anything else.

Even so, Leigh Anne had some bad days that October when Collins went through rush. After Collins made the round of sorority parties, she called Leigh Anne and said, "Mom, I had such a great time at another sorority."

Leigh Anne said, "Collins, stop right there. You're going to be a Kappa Delta and it's not optional. What part of that confuses you? I will not pay a sorority bill for anyone else. I don't *care* what any other sorority said or did." Then she hung up.

That very day, Leigh Anne drove down to Oxford. She called Michael and took him out to lunch. As they put in a huge order—enough for everyone in the football dorm—and waited for it to be filled, Michael could tell Leigh Anne was fretting and wanted to talk about something. He said, "What's wrong?"

"I'm not going to be able to get through this week of rush with Collins," Leigh Anne replied.

"Why?"

"Well, she called and said something about another sorority."

He said, "What other sorority? You mean there's another one besides KD?"

After living with us for years, the poor guy was so conditioned that he thought KD was the only sorority that existed. Or mattered.

We thought Michael might struggle with the transition to college, but we were wrong; instead it was Collins who had the first rough patch. Almost immediately, she came down with a bad case of homesickness. When the longings for home hit, Michael gave her crucial comfort. Collins's freshman dorm was right down the street from Michael's athletic dorm and she went practically everywhere with him. In the past we had counted on Collins to look out for Michael, but now there was a role reversal and Michael became Collins's protector.

One weekend in October they drove to Memphis for their first visit back home. Collins was visibly struggling with being away from us, and when we all sat down at the dining table she burst into tears.

"I don't like it there," she said, weeping. "I don't want to go back. I want to come *home*."

Sean tried to comfort her and said, "Just hang in there a little longer. If you still really hate it, you can come back."

Then Michael chimed in. "If she's coming home, I'm coming home!"

Michael was adamant: he had no intention of attending Ole Miss without Collins.

"I'm not staying there without C-Bell," he announced.

"Whoa, whoa, whoa," Leigh Anne said.

"Let's just calm down," Sean said.

"Everyone is going back to school," Leigh Anne declared.

It was a classic case of freshman blues, and they soon got over it. By February they wouldn't have come home on a bet.

Michael and Collins had always been close, but now they became inseparable. Michael helped Collins through the adjustment to a heavier college workload, and they even trained some together sometimes. Collins made varsity cheerleader as a freshman, which was a real feat since collegiate cheerleading is not just pom-poms and high kicks. It's a muscular coed performance, a combination of high-level gymnastics and dance, with partner stunts like throws twenty feet in the air followed by basket catches. It's just as demanding as a varsity sport, and the number of blown knees attests to that: torn anterior cruciate ligaments are the No. 1 injury in cheering. Collins was in the best shape of her life, at 110 pounds of solid ripping muscle, and she could keep up with Michael as they did sprints, lunges, circuits, and ran the ramps to the top of the football stadium.

But the combination of intense workouts and classes put a strain on Collins and she began to get severe migraine headaches. Initially, they were terrifying because she didn't know what they were. The first time she had one, she called Michael and he rushed over in his truck to take her to the emergency room. On the way, he dialed us from his cell phone.

"I'm taking C-Bell to the doctor. She's really sick; there's something bad wrong. Ya'll need to get down here," he said.

"Okay, we're on the way," Leigh Anne said.

All of a sudden he shouted, "Ohhhhhhhhh!"

Leigh Anne, on the other end of the line, wondered what on earth happened. All she could hear were a lot of muffled noises.

"Michael, Michael, what is it?"

"She just threw up all over my pickup truck!" he said.

Michael got her to a doctor and then drove her back to her dorm and helped her to bed. He spent the rest of the evening cleaning her vomit out of the truck. That's love.

Three weeks later, Collins got another headache. Once again Michael came to the rescue. He called again from his truck. "I'm taking her back to the doctor," he reported. "We've got to figure out what's wrong. And this time, I'm making her stick her head out the window."

Michael ordered Collins to keep her head outside of the truck the whole time he drove. She sat there quietly, her head draped out of the window, panting like a little dog.

❦

Eventually, Collins and Michael settled down, and Ole Miss became a continuation of the Tuohys' dinner table. We came down for all the big games and had exuberant Saturday tailgates in the Grove, the ten-acre parcel of lawn shaded by oak, elm, and magnolias in the center of campus. Grove tailgates were legendary affairs so elaborate that they would merit an article in *Saveur* magazine. Families and fans set up tables with silver candelbra and chafing dishes with scallop kebabs, hot crab dips, platters of fried chicken and deviled eggs, black-eyed pea cornbread, and huge mounds of beef tenderloin and baked ham.

After the games, the kids would come to our Oxford house, which we had just finished building on the edge of campus. We'd put out the leftovers and Collins would bring seven or eight of her friends from the sorority, including Anne-Claire Allen and Joanne Neighbors, as well as Whitney Gadd, Catherine Ann Herrington, Jen Lawrence, and Elizabeth Walker, who we referred to as the "803 Girls" for the address of the house they all lived in. Meanwhile, Michael would bring several of his new teammates, defensive tackle Peria (pronounced Pa-ray) Jerry and his little brother John (Baby J), Jamarca Sanford, LeMarc Armour, and Jerrell Poe. Others might follow: Allen Walker, Justin Sparks, or Preston Powers.

It was a pleasure to watch our cheerleader daughter and our football-playing son integrate that old southern campus in a way no one had quite seen before. Ole Miss was worlds more diverse than it had been back when we were in school: its student body was now 19 percent black. But the campus was still a work in progress when it came to social integration. There wasn't a black fraternity on frat row at Ole Miss until 1988 and, even then, some sorehead arsonist tried to burn it down. The Phi Beta Sigmas had become extremely popular on campus, but they rarely mingled with, say, the KDs, and there were still white fraternities that would not accept a black pledge. As an Ole Miss tutor named Bobby Nix told Michael Lewis when he was researching *The Blind Side*, if you socialized with nonwhites in the Grove or on the Square, "you get this look. It's like you have a crying baby on an airplane."

The Ole Miss student body was slowly ridding the school of symbols of the Old South, however. In 2003 the goateed southern mascot, Colonel Reb, was removed from the sidelines. We heartily agreed with the move. We'd seen the effect of the Confederate flag on people when we were in college and it wasn't good.

Just before Christmas of Collins's sophomore year, she was granted a room in the elegant KD House, an old manor home fronted by a half dozen white columns. The catch was, Collins had to move out of her dorm before it closed for the holiday. It was exam week and Collins was frantically busy studying, and she couldn't reach either of us to ask if we could come and help her. If she didn't get moved she would lose the room. She flipped open her cell, called Michael, and explained her problem. "I am so stressed," she said tremulously. Michael said, "Give me five minutes."

Collins met Michael at the front desk of her dorm.

"I brought a few of my friends," he said.

Outside, half the football team was waiting on the curb, their muscles bulging out of their sleeves. It was the fastest move in history; it took less than an hour to pack up her stuff and drive it over to the KD House. Collins knocked on the door, and her sorority sisters watched, collectively slack jawed, as the guys carried her stuff inside.

For a year, one of Collins's friends had heard her talk about her "brother" who was the same age. She was stunned to be introduced to a six-foot-five black man.

"I thought ya'll were twins," she whispered. "I never knew he was the black guy in the pictures."

Collins invited Michael's friends Jamarca and Peria to come to lunch at the KD House, as a way of thanking them. But they wouldn't accept. Collins asked them several times and each time she got the same negative reply.

Miss Sue Mitchell tutored Jamarca and Peria in the Ole Miss academic support unit, and she got wind of the fact that lunch at the KD House was an issue. Collins was always picking the guys up and taking them places if they needed a lift, and they'd often eat on the Square, the social center of Oxford where students liked to sit at various restaurants. But she couldn't get them to come to lunch on sorority row.

One afternoon after a tutoring session Miss Sue said, "Jamarca, you need to go to lunch with Collins. Think of all the things she does for you guys."

"We don't need to go over there."

"Why won't you go?"

"There's racists over there."

"Well, there may be. But there are a few everywhere. Is Collins a racist?"

"No."

"Is Anne-Claire?"

"No."

"Well, that's who you're going to be eatin' with. Go on over there. You need to do this for Collins. Let people see how we all need to get along. Make a difference and lead by example."

Jamarca and Peria finally agreed. Collins hosted Michael and his friends in the elegant KD dining room. The next day when Jamarca went to Miss Sue's office for his tutoring session, she said, "Well, did you eat at the KD house yesterday?"

"Yeah."

"Did anybody try to hang you?"

"No. But I did read one girl's lips."

Miss Sue got quiet for a second.

"What did she say?"

"She said, 'They're so *big*.'"

Miss Sue, just started laughing, but Jamarca was serious.

"Miss Sue, it's hard. You don't want anybody to take anything the wrong way. You don't want anybody to be scared of you."

It was a perfect example of the power of one. Michael, Peria, and Jamarca's lunch at the KD House was a first—and it made the second and third occasions more comfortable. Eventually, it became a regular sight to see several football players lunching at the KD House. It soon became a nonissue for all concerned, and that was the best part—because race had rarely been a nonissue at Ole Miss. The fact that it wasn't a big deal was the big deal. The campus—that small, enclosed antebellum world—took notice.

❧

Michael was privileged compared to a lot of his teammates at Ole Miss. He had already assimilated into a white private school and learned to excel. But all around him were kids in the same position he once had been in: poor young black men who had been passed along and chronically underestimated. Many were not sure if they could make it.

Miss Sue was a crucial bridge for these young men at Ole

Miss. Her experience working one on one with Michael had been a revelation to her—to help change the direction of a young man's life was more gratifying than the teaching she had done in a large classroom at county high schools. For most of her career, Miss Sue had taught average, middle-class students. The school where she taught was very much a suburban haven for people who wanted to get their children away from what they considered urban blight. Most students were average or above-average students, with parents who cared how their kids were doing. Her English courses were carefully tailored toward statewide tests. Miss Sue realized, "I'm not teaching students, I'm teaching material."

The academically superior students were going to get it, whether they had a teacher or not. She hardly needed to be in the room. "We were missing the others," she said.

Some of those "others" showed up in Miss Sue's office at Ole Miss. They had been treated as commodities, bodies without minds. Everyone wanted to see them play, but no one thought they could learn. They had basically been told, in so many words, You can play football here, but you can't succeed in the classroom. They arrived at Ole Miss to be used.

Miss Sue had one student who had never been to a single math class in high school. His teacher had instead allowed him to go to the weight room—just passed him on to get a big body on the football field and out of the classroom space. The message was: you won't ever need to count. Consequently, he had no confidence that he could do well in a classroom.

"I can't do this," he said, the first time Sue sat him down to go over problems,

"Of course you can."

His first semester grades weren't wonderful.

He said, "Miss Sue, that's not very good, is it?"

"For somebody who didn't go to high school, that's pretty dang good," she said.

Miss Sue found that nothing she'd ever done was as rewarding as watching these young men's minds emerge. They were like oyster shells, closed tight at first but, when you gave them some fundamentals and encouragement, they opened up and revealed minds like beautiful pearls. It frustrated her that so many of them had never received the kind of attention from teachers that could make the classroom a good experience.

Sue heard an inspiring story from a colleague at a Memphis county school. She was struggling with two transfer students, who had arrived from poorer urban schools. One was a discipline problem and the other simply refused to talk. The teacher decided that she would try an experiment: she would say a positive thing to each of them, every day. At the end of six weeks, the discipline problem was no longer a discipline problem. He was copying problems from the board, and he told her, "You're my favorite teacher I ever had." Sue's friend reported with relief, "I'm not sure he's going to pass, but he's taken a step toward learning." The other young man who was so silent finally spoke and told her he'd never had algebra I. The reason he was so quiet was because he didn't understand anything. He was transferred out of her class, but he returned to her homeroom every couple of days just to chat.

She proved what Sue believed: that caring teachers made a difference. When someone, anyone, was willing to give cheerfully of their emotional energy and time to a kid, it was a game changer.

❦

Of course, not everyone immediately succumbed to the exhortations of Miss Sue. But she had one crucial piece of leverage: her protégés needed to be eligible to play. Eligibility was the bait, and over time she would push them toward an actual degree. "Hey, we'll take it one step at a time," she told them.

Jamarca Sanford and Peria Jerry were freshmen from Batesville, Mississippi, a town of just seven thousand in the central hill country. There was probably not one person on campus willing to bet that either would leave Ole Miss with a college degree. Not a chance. But gradually Sue, Jamarca, and Peria became more than just teacher and students, they developed deep friendships. "I've got to make contact with these guys," she told herself. "Somebody's got to build a relationship with them. It's not going to just happen."

Sue would say to Jamarca, "You need to come back tonight at seven o'clock, so we can study for this test." He'd say, "I'm not coming." But then he'd show up, because he didn't want to disappoint her, or himself. Jamarca had an uncertain athletic future at five foot ten, and he was one incident away from being kicked off the team. But, with some confidence and the knowledge that Miss Sue cared, he hit all of his marks. And Jamarca did go on to get his degree, and he also became an Ole Miss team captain.

Some people in the athletic department warned Miss Sue that Peria Jerry would only last a semester at Ole Miss. He was a huge defensive tackle—six foot one and 294 pounds—who had fought through a year at Hargrave to get his grades up. But nevertheless there were doubters. "They didn't think he was capable," Miss Sue said, with umbrage. "Well, he's perfectly capable." After three and a half years he would be well on his way to earning a degree. Beneath his gladiatorial exterior, Peria was actually a softhearted kid who craved affection and who became devoted to Miss Sue. "I wish I could get me an adopted family," he told Michael Lewis.

The truth was, Peria, Miss Sue, Collins, Michael, and several other students and teammates were forging an adopted family of their own. They took care of one another, gave one another emotional support, had one another's backs. Each of them had reached outside of his or her comfort zone to someone else—and what a difference it made.

Another good friend of ours was Patrick Willis, a middle linebacker whose nickname was "Bam Bam" for the way he hit. Like Michael, Patrick had been a foster child as a teenager, and if anything Patrick's story was more dramatic. He came from Bruceton, Tennessee, and his mother abandoned the family when he was a baby. At age six he cooked breakfast for his three younger brothers and sisters, and by age ten he was chopping cotton to help his father pay the utility bill. When he was a teenager, Tennessee's child services removed Patrick and his siblings from their father's trailer home, citing neglect. Patrick and his siblings moved in with his high school basketball coach and math teacher, Chris Finley, and Finley's wife, Julie, a fifth-grade teacher. The Finleys finished raising Patrick despite the fact that they had nothing extra to give but love. When he graduated from high school they drove him to Ole Miss, where he made the honor roll as a freshman.

Patrick became the best linebacker at Ole Miss, winning the Butkus Award despite the fact that he played the 2006 season with a hole bored in his heart by an awful tragedy: his seventeen-year-old brother, Detris, was swimming in a flooded gravel pit in Bruceton when he was struck by cramps and drowned. Detris was a 218-pound linebacker who would probably have joined his brother at Ole Miss.

All of us considered Patrick family—he even called Jamarca his "brother." Leigh Anne was part of the travel party that drove several hours to the funeral. Collins took a lot of the guys out to buy clothes for the service, because they didn't have anything to wear. (While she was coordinating their ties, belts, shirts, and dress pants, she learned that some of them had never owned a shirt that was sized by numbers. They'd only known two sizes, L or XL.) We grieved for Patrick, who kept a picture of his brother on a chain around his neck, and we admired the way he dealt with his anguish. He told everyone that he couldn't let this "destroy two lives and not just one." That spring we tried to give him some consolation and help him in any small way we could, and he spent a lot of nights sleeping on our couch. He was drafted by the San Francisco 49ers, and he later became one of the most popular men in the league, winning awards for his community service. "Athletes have got to understand that they didn't get to where they are by themselves," he says. Patrick could have let difficult circumstances harden him, but instead he only became more giving. He has gotten to a better place.

We wanted Michael to learn to be a cheerful giver, too. On holidays we told him to invite as many kids as he wanted to come home with him. At Thanksgiving of his freshman and sophomore years, he brought twenty or twenty-five Ole Miss players for dinner. Virginia, Leigh Anne, and her aunts—

especially her aunt Sara—worked the ovens all day to feed all those hulking ballplayers and, for fun, we had a turkey egg hunt. They chased around our house looking for them like they were five-year-olds.

Michael made sure that not one teammate who was hungry or didn't have family was left behind in Oxford. And when they left Memphis they knew they were welcome to come back any time.

❦

Once the traumas of their freshman year passed, Michael and Collins had the picturesque experience at Ole Miss we had always envisioned for them. Michael was named all-American and made the honor roll, while Collins became president of the Student-Alumni Council and several other campus groups. They continued to have each other's back and to break racial barriers.

To football crowds, players can seem as remote as video-game figures. We tried to make it our mission to help even the most foam-flecked spectator understand that players were human. Once a heckler realized a player had a family, relatives, he might see that they were just people.

But we didn't always tame the savage beast known as a football crowd. One Saturday afternoon at Auburn, Collins sat up in the bleachers with her friend Anne-Claire and found herself listening to a bunch of Auburn louts scream abuse at Michael. "Hey, Seventy-four, you're fat!" She tapped one on the shoulder. She wore a button with Michael's picture on it, and she had all kinds of other Ole Miss paraphernalia on her lapels. She looked like a convention delegate.

She pointed to Michael and said, "Do you see him?"

"Yes."

"He's my brother. If you say one more thing about our football team I will make sure he comes into the stands and *hurts* you."

The guy looked at Anne-Claire to see if she was serious. "She's serious," Anne-Claire said.

Michael was such a recognizable player that he was an obvious target for abuse from notoriously obnoxious SEC fans. None were more rabid than those at Louisiana State, who, fueled by massive amounts of liquor, turned Tiger Stadium into a roaring circle of hell. His junior season we headed to Baton Rouge for the annual rivalry. It led to one of our favorite family photos.

By now Michael had become quite the sartorial character, even in his uniform. He liked to "spat" his shoes, a fashion that involved wrapping tape around his cleats until they looked like they should be worn with a tuxedo. Michael also liked to color coordinate his tape, using blue to go with his Ole Miss blue jersey. (He obviously spent too much time around his interior designer mother.)

The Ole Miss colors are both blue and red, but head coach Houston Nutt considered blue jerseys more traditional. This somewhat disappointed the players, who preferred red because it looks more vivid on the field. On the Friday night before the LSU game, Coach Nutt decided to surprise the team: they would wear blazing red jerseys.

Michael had no red tape. He called us in a panic. "I don't have any red tape to spat with! I gotta have red tape!" He was practically screaming into the phone. As Leigh Anne winced and held the receiver away from her ear, everyone in the family could hear him hollering.

"Where are you?" he said.

We were still at home in Memphis. The game wasn't until six o'clock Saturday night and we intended to fly over that morning and tailgate with Sean's sister, Sarah, and her husband, George Rosevally, who helped with Team Oher so often he could have been named cocaptain. Michael announced that we needed to leave early. We had to find him some red tape.

"Mom, I don't ask you for a lot of serious things. But this is very, *very* serious!"

We canvassed every sporting goods store in Memphis looking for red tape. We finally found a place that had some—but it was about to close. Leigh Anne offered the manager our entire fortune if he would stay open. We told him we were looking for red athletic tape, and he said, "I think I have a crate of it in the back."

"We'll take the whole box."

The next morning we hurried to the airport—where we sat on the ground, unable to take off. A small plane had failed to deploy its landing gear and came in on its belly. No one was hurt, but fire trucks and rescue vehicles blocked off all of the runways. The airport was at a standstill because of the logjam.

After an hour of staring out of the plane's window and sighing in frustration, Leigh Anne said to our pilot, "What's that over there?" She pointed to a small auxiliary road that ran parallel to the runway. It was unblocked. Leigh Anne said, "Is it big enough to taxi on?" The pilot responded that it was—and revved up the engines. We circled around the traffic, radioed the tower, and lifted off.

As soon as we landed in Baton Rouge, our cell phones started pinging. By now Michael had called us nine times, wanting to know where we were. We finally reached the stadium about forty-five minutes before game time. The phone rang again.

"Are you here? Are you here?"

"We're right around the corner."

"What corner?"

"Michael, I will get there when I get there. I can see the portal."

"What portal? What portal are you at?"

We gazed up at the ramparts. "H-2," Leigh Anne said.

"I'm coming out."

Leigh Anne started shrieking.

"You're coming out?? NO!!"

All around us were drunken, foaming, staggering, rabid LSU fans.

"These people are nuts! They will take you *out*. You will never *see* the football field!"

"I'm coming out."

He walked right out of the locker room and up the concourse, unattended. He waded through the crowd in a T-shirt, football pants with pads, and cleats. As he shouldered his way up to us, the treads of his shoes made sharp clacking noises on the concrete. LSU fans stared at him and murmured, trying to figure out if it was some kind of gag.

One inebriated southern soul said, "Damn, that looks just like Michael Oher right there."

"Awww, he ain't gonna be up here in the portals," somebody else said.

Even Michael got tickled.

Now that he was there, Leigh Anne decided to seize the opportunity for a special family moment.

"Let's take the Christmas card picture!" she said.

Michael stared at her like she was out of her mind.

"I've got Tiger Stadium behind me, and I've got my kids right in front of me. It's a *great* picture," Leigh Anne insisted.

Michael stood still for a couple of snaps and then he said, "Uh, Mom, I think I need to get back in there."

Leigh Anne handed over the crate of red tape, and Michael clattered back down the rampart into the bowels of the stadium. Michael was a cheerful giver of red tape—he passed the rolls around the locker room—and the guys used it liberally, on everything from their shoes to their sleeves. When the Ole Miss team finally rushed out on the field, they wore masses of red tape wound around them. They were so decked out they looked like Christmas packages on a joy ride. They'd used every inch.

"Well, at least I taught him to be a good sharer," Leigh Anne said.

Over the past couple of years, whether dealing with social services, the adoption process, or NCAA rules, we had encountered more than our share of bureaucratic red tape. So we were happy to see real red tape put to some good use.

⁂

Michael's and Collins's senior years felt like one long celebration, thanks to the new head football coach, Houston Nutt, who became our friend. Ole Miss went 8-4 and made it to the Cotton Bowl, and in a tumultuous game they upset a top-10 team in Texas Tech, 47–34. Michael was named an all-American, a team captain, and won the Colonel Earl "Red" Blaik Leadership Scholarship Award from the All-American Football Foundation, and too many other awards to list.

But the most uproarious celebration of all was Michael's twenty-first birthday. It became the occasion of our most creative and enthusiastic giving. In the weeks leading up to it, we told Michael to think of something he'd never done before. We offered to take him and some of his friends anywhere they wanted to go—but it had to be somewhere he'd never been. We wanted to give him a brand-new experience.

We figured Michael would want to go to Vegas. Or Atlantis. Wrong.

He wanted to ride roller coasters.

For his birthday trip, Michael asked to go to Sandusky, Ohio. We researched amusement parks and found that Sandusky was home to the Cedar Point amusement park, "The Roller Coaster Capital of the World!" Michael wanted to ride roller coasters—and Cedar Point had *seventeen of them*! Four of them were terrifying contraptions more than two hundred feet tall. Cedar Point also had a water park named Soak City, miniature golf, and go-karts.

Leigh Anne commandeered Air Taco. The travel party consisted of Michael, Jamarca, Peria, and BenJarvus Green-Ellis. BenJarvus was an All-SEC running back who had two thousand-yard seasons running behind Michael before signing with the New England Patriots, where his teammates called him "Law Firm" because of his many-syllabled, hyphenated name. Also along for the ride were Collins, Anne-Claire, and Miss Sue.

On the tarmac, Peria studied Air Taco with grave reservations. None of the guys except Michael had ever ridden on a small private plane before.

"I'm not riding on that little thing," Peria announced.

Leigh Anne said, "Get on the plane."

"No, ma'am."

"Peria, if it's your time to go, it's your time to go."

Jamarca said, "But what if it's Michael's time to go and we're just *with* him?"

"Get on the plane."

Cedar Point was a wonderland of thrill rides, spinning rides, whiplash rides, and water rides. The first thing Michael wanted to do was ride the biggest, baddest roller of all. It was called the Magnum XL-200 and it was a positively demonic-looking structure that rose two hundred feet in the air. The kids wedged themselves into the cars, which then shot out of the loading area. They made the slow cranking ascent . . . pulled up over the rise . . . and hurtled downward at a ninety-degree angle, everyone shredding their throats with their screams.

Michael was fearless. But Jamarca was scared to death, and after he got off he vowed he wasn't going to ride another. For the next couple of hours he defiantly stood flat-footed and watched as the rest of us rode the Blue Streak, the Corkscrew, the Disaster Transport, the Iron Dragon, the Mantis, the Maverick, the Wicked Twister, and the Raptor. Bobsleds plunged into darkness, and cars whirled around pretzel turns and threw us head over heels, screaming.

Michael's only disappointment that day was that he wasn't allowed on a couple of the rides because of his size— he couldn't fit the safety bar over his fifty-eight-inch chest.

He would try to wedge it down, and jam the buckle into place, until Leigh Anne hollered at him, "Do *not* force that."

Finally, just before we were ready to leave, Jamarca tentatively agreed to a last ride. The group jubilantly trouped off to the Corkscrew except for BenJarvus (who'd just had his wisdom teeth removed and couldn't take the high-speed rides), Sue, and Leigh Anne. The Corkscrew was an iron-tracked twister that spun its victims 360 degrees, upside down. Spectators could stand underneath it and watch as it coiled at high speed. Sue and Leigh Anne and BenJarvus loitered under the ride, craning necks upward, looking for the group.

Miss Sue said, "Wouldn't it be funny if that one stopped at the top?"

Then it did.

When the kids got off, Jamarca was ashen and rubber-legged and swore he'd go to no more amusement parks for the rest of his days. "My feet need to stay right here on the ground," he said. BenJarvus was bent over double with hysterical laughter, his squeals so high-pitched he sounded like a little girl.

❦

That spring was especially hectic as Michael and his teammates prepared for the NFL draft. They had to stay in peak condition while flying off to scouting combines and interviews with NFL teams. Meanwhile, Collins and her friends were also going to job interviews and trying to figure out what to do with their lives. To save money, all of them decided to move into our house in Oxford together. Just after graduation, Michael, Jamarca, and Peria took up residence along with Collins, Anne-Claire

Allen, and Joanne Neighbors. The KD House met the athletic dorm right in our living room. For four months, the entrance foyer was jammed with an assortment of sneakers, baseball caps, Chanel sunglasses, and designer handbags. It was a reality show waiting to happen.

When the day of the NFL draft arrived, it felt both like the end of something and the beginning. We all put on our best dresses and coats and ties and flew to New York to be with Michael. Also along for the celebration was our friend Jimmy Sexton, who had just become Michael's agent, and the people who were the most meaningful bookends in Michael's life—his brother Marcus, his closest childhood comrade from Hurt Village Craig Vail, and Miss Sue.

We were thrilled for Michael and, like all proud parents, we felt a wonderful sense of completion. But we also felt an almost melancholy sense of finality—we knew the draft meant the end of his childhood dependence on us. He was grown up now; he would rarely need us anymore. "It's kind of sad," Sean said.

Michael was projected as a first-round pick, which took much of the anxiety out of the day. The only question was how high he would go, and this was an issue of pride with Michael: he wanted to be the first offensive lineman chosen.

We had to wait longer than we anticipated for his name to be called. A so-called prognosticator at ESPN named Todd McShay had suggested that Michael was a character risk who had "off the field issues" and questioned his "work ethic." The statement was so inaccurate and misinformed that it should discredit McShay in perpetuity. McShay also issued a vague warning about Percy Harvin. Harvin would become the NFL Rookie of the Year. Michael would be the runner-up.

A lot of teams simply failed to recognize that Michael's past had given him nothing *but* character.

Three offensive linemen were selected among the first ten, and none of them were Michael. Next, Green Bay, San Francisco, and Buffalo all passed as well. We were unconcerned. As Sean said, "Now he's got something to prove."

"How about a game of hearts?" Leigh Anne said, as we sat down to wait at a round table backstage.

Sean passed the time by calling his friend Matt Saunders. Though Sean was almost fifty and Matt was in his late twenties, they were the closest of friends. As Leigh Anne liked to point out, "You both act like you're eighteen." Matt had recently moved on to the head coach's job at a large public school in a county outside of Memphis. Matt was about to have his first spring football scrimmage, and Sean was thinking about ways to help Matt build morale. An old Skeets Tuohy lesson about pride came back to him. "How 'bout you get the kids some T-shirts?" Sean said. "Put something inspirational on them. I'll pay for 'em." Leigh Anne thought, *That's Sean: in the middle of the NFL draft he's thinking about T-shirts for kids.*

As more draftees' names were called, the crowd in the backstage greenroom area began to thin. Suddenly, during a break in the action, NFL commissioner Roger Goodell appeared. Sean suspected he knew why he was there: the previous year ESPN had caught quarterback Brady Quinn's angst on camera as he was passed over by twenty teams, until Goodell spirited him away to a suite to suffer in private. Goodell was checking to see if anyone needed privacy.

Goodell worked his way around the Tuohy table, saying

hello. Leigh Anne didn't pay much attention because she was caught up in another conversation with a well-wisher. Sean tried to get her attention by taking her elbow. He said to Goodell, "This is my wife."

Leigh Anne, who was being pulled in two different directions, glanced absently at Goodell as she shook his hand. Then she said, "I'm sorry, who are you and what's your job back here?"

Everyone froze. Jimmy Sexton's face drained to white. Sean thought, *Oh, my God, she just insulted the commissioner and he's going to suspend Michael in revenge.*

Goodell just arched his eyebrows in amusement and said, "It's not real important who I am, and I'm not sure why I'm back here. Now I'll go back where I belong. I just wanted to make sure you are doing okay."

Jimmy said, "Everything is just fine back here."

"I can see that."

"Thank you for checking on us," Sean said.

⁂

Not long after Goodell went back onstage to announce another draft pick, Jimmy Sexton's phone rang. It was Ozzie Newsome, the general manager of the Baltimore Ravens—and the smartest man in the NFL as far as Leigh Anne was concerned. He had traded up to No. 23 in order to select Michael. Jimmy handed the phone over.

"Do you want to be a Raven?" Newsome asked Michael. "Because we're going to pick you."

Michael grinned broadly and jumped up, leaned across the

table, and gave Sean a fist bump. Out of nowhere, a bunch of Baltimore Ravens caps appeared. Michael put one on, and so did S.J. and Craig.

Onstage, Commissioner Goodell stepped to the podium. "The New England Patriots have traded the twenty-third pick to the Baltimore Ravens, and with the twenty-third pick in the 2009 NFL draft the Baltimore Ravens select . . . Michael Oher, offensive tackle, Mississippi." Was it our imagination, or did Goodell wear an especially warm expression as Michael walked across the stage to a huge ovation? (Then again, his expression might have been prompted by fear of Leigh Anne.)

Our eyes welled up as Michael accepted a Ravens jersey and a hug from Goodell. Everyone in the room knew Michael's story and was moved. But no one was more moved than Michael, who simply wept. "I had dreams about the moment, years before," he said later. "Waiting for it, I knew how hard I had worked, for so long, to get to it. I was going through so many things, it was just unbelievable. I just couldn't wait for it. It's what I've been looking for forever."

On July 30, 2009, Michael signed a multiyear contract with the Ravens worth millions. He was a made man. When someone asked Michael about the role we'd played in his life, he answered generously, "All the hard work they've put in has paid off. I'm just glad I was able to give back by making it to the NFL." But it wasn't important to us that he was a great football player. What really mattered was that he made the most of his gifts.

Michael's new status showed in his demeanor. When he walked into a room he commanded it, not just with his size but with his charisma and character. His transformation was complete—but the transformation had nothing to do with what he wore or how he played football. It had to do with what was inside of him. He had always been talented—that hadn't changed—it was his confidence that changed. All he'd ever needed was a chance, a little hope, a lot of love, and an opportunity.

Still, Michael insisted on giving back to our family. He announced that he wanted to buy S.J. a car. Like most teenaged boys, S.J. had a fixation with hot rods, and he kept a picture of a Dodge Challenger on the home screen of his laptop. Leigh Anne put her foot down. "Absolutely not," she said. S.J. had just turned sixteen; he was too young to own a car and, anyway, Michael didn't need to throw away his hard-won new money.

But Michael knew how badly S.J. wanted a car. Whenever Michael traveled he would leave his own new ride, a massive Hummer, in the care of S.J. For weeks at a stretch S.J. got to tool around Memphis in the mother of all gaudy, gas-guzzling vehicles and pretend it was his own. S.J. loved driving the Hummer so much that when Michael came home he had to pry the keys out of S.J.'s sweaty little hands. "He can't stay out of it," Michael said.

One day Michael finally told S.J. he was repossessing the car. "I'm taking the Hummer to Baltimore," he said.

"Well, okay," S.J. said, crestfallen. "I guess I don't have a car."

Michael said, "Do you really like that Dodge Challenger on your home screen?"

"Yeah, I like it."

"Do you like it in red?"

"What do you mean? Sure."

"It's yours," Michael said. "I bought it for you. All you have to do is go over and pick it up."

Leigh Anne was beside herself. "That is *ridiculous*," she said. "A little red sports car—exactly what you need at sixteen, right?" But it was done; there was no returning the car. S.J. was the proud owner of a hot red car.

We were excited to see what the future held for Michael—and for our other surrogate sons from Ole Miss, who had worked just as hard as Michael to make it to the league. Peria Jerry was the very next player selected after Michael; he went to the Atlanta Falcons. Jamarca Sanford was chosen by the Minnesota Vikings. Teammates Ashlee Palmer landed with the Buffalo Bills and Mike Wallace went to the Pittsburgh Steelers. All were young men whom we Tuohys loved and were so proud of.

Their lives were about to change rapidly—and so were ours. At the same time Michael was preparing to report to the Ravens for his first training camp, *The Blind Side* was completing production. It would be released that fall—just in time for his rookie season. We were equal parts unnerved and thrilled by the prospect but, mainly, we had no idea what to expect. We couldn't know that it would become a runaway hit, or foresee how people would respond to it, flocking to watch it in the darkness with tears streaming down their faces.

Later, after it had reached the theaters, Michael called Leigh Anne.

"Mama, I don't know why everybody cries at the movie," he said.

"What do you mean?" she said.

He started laughing. "Don't they know it has a happy ending?" he said.

INTERLUDE

Sean Junior

SON

FOR PEOPLE WHO GO IN SO MANY DIRECTIONS, WE'RE A close family. Very. Which is weird. No idea how that happened. There's no reasonable explanation, because we're at four points of the compass.

My teachers get mad at me because at school we get progress reports and the parents have to sign them, and I'm like, "My parents are out of town." They say, "Who's staying with you?" I say, "Tonight, Collins or Mike, and then tomorrow night I think one of Collins's friends will be there. My mom will be back Friday—maybe." They all freak out. I swear there's never a week when all five members of the family are in the house at one time. Never happens.

My mom is always busy decorating and my dad is always on the road with the Grizzlies, and Collins is always doing something because she has two million interests. God knows what she does. But with Mike we all kind of had to stop and do stuff together. My dad would help him study and my mom was always trying to do something for him, so we were all in one place at the same time.

Growing up, it was like I always had a brother. For Collins, she grew up most of her life and *then* Mike came. For me, I grew up *with* Mike. He was the brother I never had and the brother I always had. Anyway, I loved it.

Mike worked so hard in high school—I swear, I lost two hours of sleep a night. I'd go to bed at like ten, and I'd wake up at two in the morning because Sue would be yelling at him to stay awake. When Sue didn't wake me up, I woke up anyway. It's not like he was Mr. Nimble sneaking past my bed. Mike going up the stairs sounds like a freaking bookcase falling over.

He always had to be the first one at school—that was his rule for himself—so he'd get up at five or six in the morning. Now that I'm in high school I'm like "How did he do that?" Because there's no way. As a sophomore, I think I have actually set the record for the most tardies in Briarcrest history. I'm going to see if I can hit triple digits next year.

Mike and I hung out a lot because we shared rooms. I always knew when he was going to practice and I'd say, "Can I go with you?" He'd say, "Come on, then." He took care of me a lot when my parents were out of town. We'd go eat. We'd go to Subway, better known as "Suway" to Michael. ("Bs" are optional for him.) He was a big fan of Perkins, where you can get like seven plates of food for ten dollars. We would go to P.F. Chang's more than any family should. They should name the chicken-and-shrimp fried rice after him.

Sometimes we would just keep it simple with the free Taco Bell. Getting free Taco Bell is a *huge* deal now that I am in high school. Every now and then we would go to the competition, better known as McDonald's, and Mike could put away some Big Macs. At Moe's Southwest Grill, they have the perfect meal, called the Joey Bag, for $9.87. (Though I get it for $4.43 because me and the manager are pretty tight, that's my guy.) Every tenth time you get a free burrito.

The thing about the movie is that it shows Mike's early, early years. Now he's Mister Personality. He's almost a genius, as far as just being able to read people, his social skills, and his survival instincts. He's a lot like my dad; he can figure anything out in two seconds. I can't even explain it. Also, he can remember things from years ago. He'll say, "Remember when I first came here, and we played Xbox for the first time?" It was like seven years ago. He'll say, "You were the Bucks and I was the Magic, and I beat you 97–94."

I'm like, "Yeah, sure. I guess. Maybe."

He also has a selective memory. Which can be good, and bad, and funny. We'll have some sort of family discussion about a vacation we took, and he'll chime in about how great it was. None of us really bother to tell him that he wasn't around when that happened.

In our house if you want something, you got to work for it, unfortunately. My parents don't just give it to you. People always say to me, and it really, really, gets to my dad, "You're just a rich kid." You know, he worked his butt off. He was nothing growing up. That rich kid stuff, that's the crap that everyone gives you, but it doesn't bother me. Sure. I'll take it.

People will always have something to say and, mostly, they don't know anything about it. When it comes to people who think negatively about my family, I take the mind-over-matter policy: I don't mind, and you don't matter. Get over it.

Let me describe my parents. My dad is the most sarcastic person in the world. Very funny in his own mind. He's real quick, smart, he always knows a solution to everything. He has me cracking up 24/7. He is a competitor, even if he's playing checkers with a five-year-old, he is going after the win. He isn't one of the most social members of the family, though. He usually wins the award for family ass——. (Don't worry, I am allowed to say ass, by the way . . . it's in the Bible.)

My mom has a heart of gold, but you definitely don't want to get on her bad side. She is a very charitable person. Not a big culinary person. She *tries* to do the right thing; she always has good intentions. But she could yell at a wall. I think yelling is a big-time hobby of hers and she has mastered it. She's the type that will cuss at you for cussing.

Both of them have their tempers. Both, when they get their minds made up, it's set and it's not changing.

They're good parents—not the worst. You know, *The Blind Side* is a story people choose to tell, but it's not the only story like that. I get messages on Facebook all the time from people; they send me two pages about things that happened to them, stories that are way better. Last year my mom and dad got this award for Parents of the Year, basically because Michael got drafted by the NFL and became a millionaire. As if three years earlier they were crappy parents? You know, it's a bunch of publicity that may or may not be deserved.

When the movie came out, Collins, Michael, and I put some of our money together and gave it back to our church. Then Collins bought like seven purses. Mike bought rims for his car and then a month later got tired of those rims and bought new rims. Me? I was the only one who put my money in the bank. It's still in there. Minus a couple hundred bucks I took out to buy some Ray-Bans.

My mom keeps saying life is going to turn back to normal at some point. But I'll believe it when I see it. I don't think it'll ever be a hundred percent the same, because now all eyes are on the Tuohys. There's no margin for error. It isn't so bad, though. I welcome the challenge. I can handle myself just fine. My mom says, "Don't screw up or it will be a reflection on this whole family."

I just say, "Yes, ma'am."

6

Blindsided

Do small things with great love.

—LEIGH ANNE TUOHY

WE COULDN'T SEE ANYTHING VERY CINEMATIC ABOUT our family life. It struck us as more of a cable reality show than a movie. Also, we had our reservations about a motion picture because, as far as we could tell, Hollywood's idea of a true-to-life portrayal of a Southerner was an actor with a phony hee-haw accent saying, "Pa, pass me another bowl of grits."

Nevertheless, John Lee Hancock assured us he could turn *The Blind Side* into a good film. John Lee was a tall, bespectacled Texan who had studied at Baylor before he became a writer-director, and his vision of Michael Lewis's best-seller was smart and inspirational. He saw mass appeal in the relationship between Michael and Leigh Anne, though he warned us that he didn't intend to sugarcoat Michael's life or turn Leigh Anne into Mother Teresa.

"I'm not about making you look worse than you actually are," he said, "but I'm also not about making you look better than you actually are."

John Lee was so frank and genial that we felt safe in his hands. And, in the end, he took only a little artistic license in his script. In his version, Collins played volleyball. She didn't react to that well. She said in a flat, disdainful tone of voice, "Volleyball. Really?"

We also had faith in the producer of the film, Gil Netter. He and John Lee never wavered in their conviction about what the movie should be. Obviously, they knew what they were doing.

One morning, John Lee called and said he had offered the lead role to Sandra Bullock, which we found very flattering. But he added that Sandra had hesitated to accept it and wanted to know if she could come to Memphis to meet Leigh Anne before she made up her mind.

Leigh Anne could just envision the carnival that came along with a visit from an actress.

"She's welcome to come, but you need to understand something," Leigh Anne said. "I can't do limos. I can't do nine assistants. That's just not how we roll. If Sandra Bullock wants to come by herself and jump in the sandbox with us, bring her on."

A couple of days later, Leigh Anne opened the front door to meet an unadorned, self-effacing woman; she was wearing capri slacks, had a ponytail and very little makeup, and was unaccompanied by handlers. After she introduced herself, Leigh Anne was surprised to realize that Sandra was tense.

"Are you nervous?" Leigh Anne asked.

"I am."

"Why are you nervous?"

"I don't know, but I am."

"Well, it's fine, you either like me or you don't like me. So come on in and analyze, me, or whatever it is you want to do, and then go and figure it out."

Later that day, Leigh Anne drove Sandra to Oxford to show her Ole Miss, and got to like her even better. When they went to lunch Leigh Anne half expected Sandra to ask for "purified water" or "organic soy cheese," but instead she happily dove into a plate of fried food. That was who she was—low maintenance, unpretentious, and, as we discovered, a bit of a smart aleck, which meant she fit in fine. Ironically, Sandra once said that she didn't like the Academy Awards show, because "I'd rather roll home, put on the jeans, go outside, pick up dog poop, or go for a run or something." She fell right in step with our family.

We also shared similar sensibilities about giving, especially to kids. After Hurricane Katrina hit New Orleans, Sandra adopted the Warren Easton Charter High School, which had sustained $4 million in damages. She donated hundreds of thousands of dollars for renovations, built a new health clinic, bought new band uniforms, and established a ten-thousand-dollar scholarship. Today she's still giving to the school, and to New Orleans. As Warren Easton's principal said, "She acts as if all eight hundred–plus of these children are her own."

Our kind of girl.

It was on the drive back from Oxford that Sandra got up her nerve to ask if Leigh Anne actually carried a gun. Leigh

Anne popped the console between the seats and showed her a little hand pistol. She said, "Ya'll need to carry one of these."

After that, Sandra apparently called John Lee and said, "Leigh Anne terrifies me, but I think I have to play this role." She had overcome her reservations about Christian proselytizing, too. We took it as a great compliment when Sandra told us she admired our faith. "You walk your walk," she said. Then she added, "You're the first Christians I've met who haven't judged me, or did one thing and said another."

The Blind Side finally started filming in April 2008 in Atlanta, backed by a company named Alcon Productions. The person we had to thank for shepherding it was a young executive producer named Molly Smith, who we knew well. Molly is the daughter of Fred Smith, the founder of FedEx, and we had little doubt she'd make a success of the film. She'd worked her way up in the business after graduating from NYU film school and had a record of translating good books into good films. Plus, she'd inherited her family's entrepreneurial talent. Her great-grandfather was a steamboat captain and her grandfather was a partial founder of the Greyhound bus system. As for Fred, everyone knew his legendary story: the idea for FedEx had started as his college thesis and he'd spent years struggling to build the company.

By now we considered all of the people involved in *The Blind Side* friends. We saw a lot of Gil Netter, and he and Sean even took fly-fishing trips together. But it was still an uncomfortable sensation to have our family rendered on film. We were deeply grateful for his commitment to keeping the story true. Sandra was so concerned about getting the part right that she had questions almost every day—sometimes three times a day—for five straight months. She worked with a dialect coach, and she asked Leigh Anne what labels she wore and what shade of makeup. John Lee even sent a film crew to our house so he could get the decor right.

Leigh Anne didn't see what should be so hard about playing her in a movie, because she thought Sandra had a lot of the same qualities, chiefly spunk and a quick mouth. But gradually we came to understand what a difficult job it was to keep the screen character from coming off as a cartoon, "all schmaltzy and soft," as Sandra put it. She also explained how many people and moving parts went into a film and how little quality control she actually had.

Leigh Anne appreciated the film crew's attention to detail. But then one night Sandra said to John Lee, "Text Leigh Anne and find out what kind of nightgown she wears."

John Lee just stammered, "Ahhhhh . . ."

He knew what kind of reply he was likely to get from Leigh Anne, but he texted her anyway. Leigh Anne immediately responded with a one-sentence reply:

"Ya'll need to get a life."

❦

To Michael, the movie was a distraction. He was less interested in who he had been than in who he wanted to become. He was trying to prove himself as a player and he didn't want anyone thinking he was more interested in red carpets than the football field.

"I don't want to be different," he told Leigh Anne. "I don't want any special treatment. I just want to play football."

One day Leigh Anne found an opportunity to buttonhole

the Ravens' safety Ed Reed in the team hotel. Leigh Anne knew Ed could relate to Michael, because when he was a teenager his family had struggled financially and for a time he had lived with his assistant high school principal, who he considered almost a second mother.

"Don't you let anyone make fun of Michael in the locker room," Leigh Anne said.

"No, ma'am," Ed said. "I'm kind of adopted, too. I hope this movie helps a lot of kids."

Nevertheless, from the time Michael attended his first rookie camp in Baltimore there was buzz about the movie. "You going to be on TNT?" guys razzed him. Michael tried to preempt the teasing by making it clear that he wasn't out to be a personality; he wanted to be a pro.

Michael's rookie season became yet another excuse for our family to gather around a dinner table—only we took the table on the road. Sean bought Ravens season tickets and handpicked box seats after carefully surveying Alliance Bank Stadium. He walked around the rim and up and down the stadium stairs, looking for the best vantage point from which we could watch the offensive line, before settling on four seats in the club level, section 203. Michael was named the starter at right tackle for the season opener against the Kansas City Chiefs, and we piled into Air Taco to go see him play.

Leigh Anne had heard all about how rough NFL crowds could get, and so she decided to have a "Come to Jesus" meeting with the people seated around us in section 203. She wanted to get a few things straight right from the start. Leigh Anne stood up and called for their attention. "Here we go, guys," she said, clapping.

"Let me tell you something, I'm Michael Oher's mom," she announced. "Now, we're all going to get along; we're going to hold hands. There's going to be no booing, no cussing, and, after the third quarter, no drinking. And if ya'll act like jerks the whole time, it's going to be a two or three drink maximum."

The other spectators stared at her with their mouths hanging open. Still, they seemed to buy into the deal.

Not that anything they said or did would have upset Sean. He was so focused on the game that he kept earphones in his ears so he wouldn't have to talk to anyone. The wire wasn't connected to anything in his pocket. In true Sean fashion, he just stuck the plugs in his ears so no one could bother him.

The Ravens beat the Chiefs, 38–24, and it was the first of a series of remarkable rookie performances for Michael. He started all sixteen regular season games; later in the fall he moved over to the more crucial left tackle position, and then flipped back and forth, which meant he had to master two positions in the same season. Even with our binoculars, we couldn't keep up with which side of the field he was on.

Michael helped the Ravens gain their second-highest offensive yardage total in franchise history—but he still couldn't quite believe what was happening to him. "I was in awe," he said later.

He told us that each week he'd go up to one of the players on the field and say, "I'm just happy to be out here with you." Then on the next play, "they'd try to kill me."

We went to every game, including those on the road. We were around the team so much that we gradually became acquainted with Michael's coaches and teammates. When the

Ravens played at San Diego, Leigh Anne got a chance to meet quarterback Joe Flacco. Or rather, she accosted him.

That Saturday night at the team hotel they stepped into an elevator together. Leigh Anne turned to him and said, "I'm Michael Oher's mom. You need to get rid of the ball faster."

Fortunately, Flacco thought it was kind of funny. After a moment, he said, "Yes, ma'am, I do."

The next day as they were dressing for the game in the locker room, Flacco sought out Michael. "Hey, Mike. Your mom is coming up to me in the elevator and saying I need to get rid of the ball faster."

Michael said, "Oh my God."

After the game, Michael found Leigh Anne. "Mom. You can't be saying things like that."

"Okay, I'm sorry," she said. "But he needs to get rid of it faster."

Now it was Leigh Anne's turn to seek out Flacco. She went looking for him. "Where's the tattletale?" she demanded. "Where's he at?" When she found him, she said, "You're just a big baby."

Over the next several games, after a good deal of jaw-jacking back and forth, Joe and Leigh Anne settled into a friendly relationship.

But for all of Leigh Anne's truculence, Michael's rookie season was a deeply emotional experience for her, as it was for all of us. Each time he was introduced in the starting lineup, when the loudspeaker boomed his name and he ran onto the field, Leigh Anne would burst into tears. When we analyzed why it touched us so much, we realized that of all the things Michael gave us, perhaps the greatest gift was hope. Watching him on the field gave us hope that others like Michael could emerge from their desolate, dead-end circumstances. It gave us hope that people's lives could be changed. It gave us hope that we could make a little bit of a difference.

❦

Millions of others apparently felt the same. With the release of *The Blind Side* came an explosion of publicity. The film premiered in New York in October, and then opened nationwide on November 20. But Michael skipped the premiere—he never broke his vow to be a football player, not a personality. The Ravens had a Monday night game on the road that week, and the premiere was on a Tuesday night. He was just as happy to miss it.

"It was my first year in the NFL and I was playing a lot and I'm a guy that once I set my mind to something, I'm going to do it," he said later. "I just wanted to stay focused. I didn't want to go to any movie premieres or be a celebrity or anything like that."

Perhaps just as important, he was also self-conscious about how his fellow players and opponents would receive the film. "I just wanted to see how my teammates were going to take it and how the people I'm playing against were going to take it," he said.

When Michael finally saw *The Blind Side*, he did it quietly, on the sly. One afternoon he and a couple of friends simply walked up to a box office, bought tickets, and slipped into their seats in a darkened theater. "I watched it and thought it was a good movie, and just went on from there," he said.

While *The Blind Side* gathered steam at the box office, Michael was coming into his own as a player. It was a ritual for the Ravens to stop at the player exit after every game and sign autographs. Crowds packed the barricades and would holler out their names, hoping to lure them over for a signature. We would wait by the car for Michael to finish, and eventually the fans began to recognize us as Michael's family. One evening, some rather overserved fans began to whistle at Collins.

"Collins, we want to marry you!"

"Hey, Michael, your sister's hot!"

Michael said, "Collins, go get in the car."

"They're just drunk," Collins said.

Michael turned to his good friend and teammate, Ray Rice. "Ray, you take her."

Collins shook her head. "I'm a big girl, Michael, I can take care of myself. Like I'm going to accept one of their proposals?"

Ray stepped forward and took Collins by the elbow.

"Ray, he's not the boss of you, you don't have to do what he says," Collins said.

"He protects me, I protect you," Ray said, and steered her firmly toward the car.

The Ravens went 9-7 in the regular season and thrilled us every week; five of their losses came by just a touchdown or less. Michael and his teammates on the offensive line knocked down opponents like bowling pins. They helped Ray Rice to 2,271 yards rushing, and a franchise-record twenty-two rushing touchdowns (tied for most in the NFL). When Michael was mentioned as a candidate for Rookie of the Year along with Percy Harvin, Leigh Anne was exultant. She kept thinking about those teams that had passed on him in the draft. "They're all kicking themselves over Michael, and I love it," she said. "Every single guy who passed on him should be fired."

The Ravens made the play-offs and accomplished a huge upset by knocking off New England, 33–14, in part because they got off to a great start on Ray Rice's eighty-three-yard touchdown run. That drew them a meeting with Peyton Manning and the Indianapolis Colts in the divisional round. We had high hopes for another upset, but it turned out to be a dispiriting afternoon, as they suffered a 20–3 season-ending loss.

As the game wore on, a Colts fan seated a row in front of us became drunk and abusive toward Michael. He would stand up and shout down at the field, "Hey, Blind Side! You suck!"

After a while Collins grew weary of listening to him exercise his vocal cords. She leaned over and grabbed him by the collar.

"You say that one more time, I'm going to make sure Blind Side comes up here and beats the crap out of you. That's my brother."

The drunk just sort of bobbed his head at Collins in amazement.

"*Not* kidding," she said. "That's my brother. I will have him kill you."

"Okay, okay," he said. "I apologize."

After the guy sat back down, we said to Collins, "Did you have to?"

"I wasn't going to listen to that the whole game," Collins said.

The acorn didn't fall far from the tree.

❦

We were exhilarated by the success of *The Blind Side*, but it didn't come without emotional complications for us as a family.

We discovered that not everyone was necessarily inspired by us. Along with newfound celebrity came critics who found something wrong with the film, or who questioned our motives.

S.J. caught a lot of flak for all of us. He was extremely visible at Briarcrest, sometimes uncomfortably so as he experienced his share of hazing. It's traditional among the Memphis high school student bodies to chant back and forth at each other during games, and sometimes the banter got pretty creative. You can imagine what a bunch of rivalrous adolescents did to S.J. over *The Blind Side.* As soon as he took the basketball court for the 2009–2010 season, he started hearing it.

"Your dad should've adopted a point guard because you stink!"

"You're only on the team because you're in a movie!"

Mostly he laughed at it—and at times it really was funny. One of Briarcrest's rivals is Memphis University School, a large elitist all-boys private academy. Their colors are red and blue, after Harvard and Yale, which tells you a little bit about their pretensions. The rivalry can get pretty hot. This season Briarcrest went to MUS for a game, and by the midpoint of the game, Briarcrest was ahead. The Briarcrest students chanted, "This is our house!"

The MUS section chanted back, "You can't afford it!"

When S.J. took the floor to run the point, the MUS students chanted, "Tu-ohy's Mon-ey!"

But the Briarcrest section had S.J.'s back. They chanted:

"Free-ee Taco Bell!"

MUS had no reply to that.

Then some boys started chanting, "Can you get us a date with Sandra Bullock?"

You can imagine how Leigh Anne, sitting up in the stands, dealt with it. She seethed. "That's ridiculous!" she'd say. "I'm going to punch someone!"

Later on, she told S.J., "You should just shoot 'em the bird."

"That's not going to work," S.J. said.

It never really stopped all season long. In another game, S.J. took a charge and hit the floor. He overdramatized the fall, hoping to get the ref to blow his whistle. "I flopped, I admit it," he said later. Though the opponent barely brushed him, down he went, and as the whistle shrieked, the opposing fans booed furiously. When S.J. ran back down the court, they chanted:

"Nice job, San-dra!"

Even S.J. had to laugh at that one.

In another game against a rival county school, S.J. got dunked over. It was a two-on-one fast break, and the guy caught it in the air and slammed it over his head. As the place erupted, S.J. heard the students singing, "Watch . . . your . . . blind side!"

"It just never ends, the humor," S.J. said later.

But S.J. handled all of the jibes. He just let them slide off, and never lost his composure. We were supremely proud of him for that.

If any of us struggled with unwanted attention from the movie, it was Michael. For him, the popularity of *The Blind Side* was especially double-edged: on the one hand it was a boon for him, because how many offensive linemen had endorsement and speaking opportunities? On the other hand it saddled him with distractions, and a preconception about who he was. What some people failed to recognize about Michael was how much he'd changed and matured over the years. We all do between the ages of fifteen and twenty-three.

"I think he's proud of where he's come from and what he's been able to accomplish, the Tuohys as his family and what they mean to him," Ravens coach John Harbaugh said. "I also think, like all of us, he wants to move on and move forward with his life. That's really the story to me, to us. It's a great motivational story for anybody, but, at the same time, what is he going to do from here on out?"

The same was true off the field. Letting go of a child can be difficult for any parent, but in our case the issue of emancipation was particularly loaded. We both still had an impulse to caretake Michael, after eight years of extremely involved parenting. It had become habit, just as it had with Collins and S.J. For example, Leigh Anne still checked their cell phones.

But now we realized that there was one more gift we could give Michael, something very important yet intangible: space. He needed room to establish his independence and a separate identity.

For the most part, Michael remained largely unaffected by his new status as the subject of a film, and an NFL player. He stayed true to his values. For instance, one of the people to whom Michael remained closest was Miss Sue, to whom he constantly tries to give back. Right before Thanksgiving he called her up and said, "I need you to come up here." She said, "I'll be there," and went to Baltimore to visit him for a few days. In fact, each of the NFL rookies from Ole Miss invited Miss Sue to come see them play that season. When she went to Minnesota to visit Jamarca, he introduced her to his teammate Adrian Peterson by saying, "This is Miss Sue. She's just like my mom."

Sue was still the teacher, and they were still her star pupils. But like the rest of us, Sue had to learn to treat Michael as an independent adult, and not as a college student anymore. Old habits were hard to break, and she constantly caught herself still trying to lecture him. Once, he said something about taking a train from Baltimore. She said, "Are you talking about the engineer or the conductor?"

"I know the difference, Miss Sue."

"I'm sorry, Michael."

❧

For the most part all three of our children dealt with the success of *The Blind Side* in the right spirit. We believed more than ever, "Unto whom much is given, much is required." Each of the Tuohy kids gave away one quarter of what they earned from Hollywood.

We impressed on them that they now had a large responsibility on their shoulders. They were all in the public eye, and it was up to them to be good stewards of their story, and to take care of its meaning.

"We want you to grasp that there is a message and a mission here, and that there is work to be done," we said.

Contrary to popular belief, the movie did not wildly enrich us. We had no participation in the profits; we only received a fee for selling our name rights to Alcon, which all in all was not a large amount. We divided it five ways.

When the movie checks came in, Leigh Anne said, "Okay, what's everybody going to do with their money?" We were not going to just keep it.

S.J. decided to donate a portion of his money to our church,

Grace Evangelical, but directed that it be used specifically in blighted Memphis neighborhoods, and that he be allowed to track it. He said, "I don't care what you do with it, as long as it's inner city, and I can follow what happens to it." The request had to be considered, because normally you can't earmark funds. He received occasional updates on how the money was spent: some of it bought tennis shoes for a public school team, and some went to emergency aid for a family. We thought it was a lovely gesture and we also contributed, as did Michael and Collins.

But Collins was not satisfied with just tithing to the church, and she looked for something additional to do with herself and her money. She gave some to the philanthropic arm of the KD sorority. She was casting around for another cause when a well-known Memphis altruist named Joe Birch stepped in and influenced her thinking.

Joe Birch is an Emmy-winning coanchor of Action News on WMC-TV in Memphis, but he's just as well known as an activist. He made a highly regarded series called "Taking Back Our Neighborhoods," which looked for solutions to problems in local communities. He raised $70,000 for St. Jude's Hospital, and after 9-11 he raised $527,000 for the United Way of New York City. But he also makes small contributions every day in Memphis. For instance, each week since 1997, Joe has delivered Meals on Wheels.

Joe gave Collins one of the most affecting days of her life when he took her with him on a delivery ride. Joe chatted easily with the people he and Collins brought food to: there was Too Tall Joe who wore a size-twenty shoe, and an elderly lady named Miss Sally. At each stop Joe paused and asked after the people who lived there, instead of just dropping the food off and walking away. It didn't take an enormous investment of time to make someone feel acknowledged, Collins realized. Joe wasn't saving anybody's life; he was just valuing them as people. And it was obvious they loved him for it.

When they were done, Joe drove Collins back to the Meals on Wheels headquarters, via a main artery called Poplar Avenue, a broad four-lane boulevard lined with high-end malls and restaurants. As they paused at a stoplight, Joe said almost casually, "You know, I have a saying: 'People need to jump off of Poplar.'"

"What does that mean?" Collins asked.

"It means sometimes you should make a left or a right and get off the Poplar corridor," Joe said. "Poplar is your comfort zone, and you need to get out of it sometimes. One day, just turn. Try it. Drive a couple of miles to the left or the right, and see what else is out there."

That was all Joe said. Yet it was one of the most powerful ideas Collins had ever heard. She sat in the passenger seat nearly immobilized by a realization: she had lived in Memphis her whole life, and she'd never taken another route, never once thought about getting off Poplar.

It was a lot like the room in Bridge Builders, when all the kids had taken a step to the left or the right. It was a visual: instead of driving in the same straight line every day, why not take a step off to the side and see what is on some other street?

❧

Collins decided to jump off Poplar—and the jump took her all the way out to Frederick Douglass High School in North Memphis.

Douglass is in one of the poorest zip codes in Memphis, but it has a rich history. The neighborhood was orginally founded by an emancipated slave named William Rush-Plummer, who became a noted reverend. Rush-Plummer was given forty acres of land by his former owner, who also happened to be his father, and on it Rush-Plummer founded a black community with a church called "Need More," so named because it needed more of everything: chairs, pews, and people.

The neighborhood, which was virtually 100 percent black, was surrounded by rail tracks to the north, south, and west. For many years, residents couldn't get out of the community on certain days of the week because they would be obstructed by stalled railroad cars. People were sometimes killed trying to cross the tracks by foot or by car. The residents lobbied for an overpass, without success. Over the years the area was also polluted by several plants and factories, which found the location convenient for loading docks tied to the rails.

Nevertheless, it was a neighborhood with intense civic pride. Residents planted community gardens, and Douglass Park was a haven where local kids could go to summer camp. Frederick Douglass High School was established in 1946, named in recognition of Rush-Plummer's admiration for the nineteenth-century abolitionist. Douglass's graduates were so devoted that they formed an alumni association with seven chapters as far-flung as Dallas, Chicago, Cleveland, Detroit, and Atlanta.

But then came the 1970s and busing. Douglass enrollment plummeted as African-American students were bused out, but no white kids bused in. In 1981, Douglass closed, and the building became a storage facility. It fell into disrepair and soon became a harbor for gang activity and spooky night adventures for local kids.

For twenty-seven years, neighborhood residents lobbied to have Douglass reopened. They even held conventions to discuss strategies for reviving it. Finally, they got their wish. In 2006, the old building was torn down to make way for a new state-of-the-art institution. On the day of demolition, Douglass alumni held a parade and pulled bricks from the rubble of the old school to keep as treasured souvenirs of their years there. A thousand people attended the groundbreaking ceremony for a school that never should have closed in the first place.

Douglass High was resurrected in the fall of 2008 with seven hundred students and sixty classrooms. Serving on the new faculty was Liz Marable, which guaranteed our interest in the school. From Liz we heard enthusiastic reviews of Douglass's innovative curriculum: it offered an elective four-year program in community and public service, in which students would learn how to become effective activists through partnerships with the city and county governments, and organizations like the United Way, Ronald McDonald House, and the Assisi Foundation. The idea was to teach kids "who they are and what their mission should be." As Douglass's gifted new principal, Janet Ware Thompson (another alum of the school), said, "We have a strong history and we wanted a dynamic education to go along with that history."

When *The Blind Side* came out we arranged a screening for the entire Douglass student body and faculty. We rented out the Malco Paradiso, a movie palace in East Memphis, and one morning in December 750 students and teachers trooped inside and took their seats, pausing at the concession stand for free popcorn and sodas. Sean got up onstage and briefly addressed the kids. "The thing you need to understand about Michael Oher," Sean told them, "is that he did *every single thing* asked of him."

As we milled around in the lobby of the Paradiso and visited with the faculty, Collins asked, "Who's the cheerleading coach?"

A teacher said, "We don't really have one."

Collins said, "Well, do you want me to help out?"

With that, Collins jumped off Poplar—and onto the Douglass bandwagon. Our daughter, the former Kappa Delta and Ole Miss cheerleader, became the volunteer cheerleading coach at Douglass High in north Memphis. Two to three days a week she went waltzing over there in her knee-high suede boots to show the girls how to tumble and high kick until they complained, "Our legs are so sore."

Collins discovered on a weekly basis how the things she took for granted often represented huge opportunities to the Douglass kids. The Douglass senior class was full of bright seventeen-year-olds whose teachers encouraged them to look at all the best universities. One day Collins asked one young lady on the cheerleading team, "What are you doing about applying to colleges?"

"I'm applying to five," she said. "I'd like to apply to five more, but I can't afford it."

This young woman had to put a cap on her applications because of the fees, which cost anywhere from twenty-five to fifty dollars each, depending on the school. Universities might offer her a rich array of financial aid packages, but this talented senior couldn't explore her opportunities as fully as she wanted to because she didn't have the cash to apply to all of them. She described the difficult decisions she was trying to make—should she apply to Vanderbilt, or the University of Tennessee? Collins thought, *This kid is going to have to give up on an opportunity over a paltry twenty-five dollars.* She would always wonder whether she could have gotten into certain schools, because she couldn't afford to pay twenty-five dollars.

"It's the popcorn theory," Collins said, when she told us about it. "It's right in front of you."

That was the sort of realization you made when you got out of your comfort zone and jumped off Poplar.

We've become big rooters for the Douglass Red Devils, whose colors are maroon, red, and white. There are increasingly frequent Tuohy sightings at Douglass. In the midst of all those students filing through the halls you might catch a glimpse of a high heel and the flash of an earring. That would be Leigh Anne, charging around, making sure people are dressed right. Leigh Anne, as usual, took charge of the clothing issue. She arranged for the track team to have two sets of singlets, red ones for home, and white for away—and she made sure that the order included sports bras that were color coordinated. She's still dressing everybody's underneath side.

Douglass High seems to us a vital project. Not every child can be Michael Oher; they can't all be plucked and taken out of their lousy circumstances. The reality is that many Memphis children will have to fight their way toward a future on their own. They will have very little help, other than the teaching and encouragement they receive at school—and at nearly every turn in Memphis is another public high school that mirrors Douglass.

On May 15, 2010, Douglass held its first graduation ceremony in twenty-nine years. It was a triumphant day: 112 of 118 members of the senior class received degrees. The school exceeded the national graduation rate by more than 20 percent. And yet, the faculty was disappointed—they had hoped for a graduation rate of 100 percent. We Tuohys take great pride in being a small part of this accomplishment, and we hope that Douglass will continue to rise above expectations.

✿

It should come as no surprise to anyone that Mister and Missus Tuohy did not observe decorum at the Eighty-second Annual Academy Awards. We vowed to be on our best behavior because we didn't want to embarrass our friend Sandra on her big night by acting like hillbillies. But the staggeringly long lines at the security checkpoints exhausted our patience. The guards examined every little lamé clutch bag as if it might contain a Stinger missile. Finally Leigh Anne lost it and started lecturing all of Tinseltown in a loud voice.

"Terrorists are *not* going to blow up the Oscars. Ya'll are just *not* that important," she said to no one in particular. "This is *not* Baghdad. That sign up there says 'Hollywood.'"

It was easier to get into the White House than it was to the Kodak Theatre, Leigh Anne went on to point out. When we finally reached the red carpet, some interviewers stopped us to chat. Leigh Anne was stewing over how much more efficiently the Academy Awards would be run if she were in charge.

"This is a long run for a short slide," she told some members of the press. "It's a lot of stuff that's not necessary if you ask me. Interesting, is all I got to say. Very friendly and very fun, and mostly very interesting."

Sean tried to gloss over his wife's remarks. "We really are having fun," he said.

Leigh Anne said, "They keep telling me, smile and act like you're having fun. Am I doing it yet?"

But once the show began, we were enchanted. It was so dazzling that we almost forgot how tense we were for Sandra. She had waited and worked for so many years and we desperately wanted her to be recognized for her performance, and for the time and tenacity she put into it.

When the envelope was finally torn open and Sandra's name was called, Sean clamped his hand hard on Leigh Anne's leg. He held it there in a death grip, which was his way of saying "Don't you dare move." He knew she was tempted to leap out of her seat and start whooping and hollering like a redneck, and he was determined to stop her. His hand stayed there throughout Sandra's wonderful speech, squeezing the blood out of her limb. Sandra's was the best speech of the night, in the unbiased view of the Tuohy family, and, somehow, Leigh Anne refrained from interrupting the big moment with her big mouth.

"I behaved like a southern lady," she said later, as if she were the queen of self-control.

Afterward, we went to the Governors Ball, where we gazed around the room at various celebrities. "They all like themselves the most," Sean murmured to Leigh Anne. But when Tyler Perry appeared, we both dropped our cool. Tyler Perry had done a lot of good work for kids in various cities, and he was one of our heroes. Sean said to him, "I want to kiss you." Tyler laughed and said, "Whoa." We got to talk to him for ten minutes uninterrupted, which was the highlight of the evening, other than Sandy's big win.

Sean further distinguished himself at the Governors Ball by swapping the place cards so that we could sit with Tim McGraw and Faith Hill, who had become friends of ours. Faith and Tim were stranded at another table with people they didn't know, so Sean actually swapped two place cards. Two gentlemen from the other table looked at Sean sourly as he made the switch. They turned out to be honchos from Warner Bros.

"It's not like I'm going to be back here next year," Sean said, grinning.

❦

Now that our children are almost grown, we're frequently asked, "What's next?" With Michael and Collins safely launched into adulthood and S.J. well on his way, where will the next piece of popcorn pop up?

One piece of popcorn is a plane ticket to Israel for Leigh Anne's mother, Virginia. Leigh Anne is struggling to be cheerful about the gift, because tours of Israel can be hot and arduous, and Leigh Anne isn't sure Virginia should put herself through it. But she's longed to go for so many years that we're sending her.

"Here's the deal," Leigh Anne told her. "If you die over there, I'm not bringing you home. Understand that. I will have you cremated and sprinkle you over the Garden of Gethsemane or someplace, which is *fine*. Because I'm not paying to bring you back. So go, kick your heels up and enjoy it. It's a lot of walking in the Holy Land and I don't think it's good for you, so if you expire over there, let it be known that you're staying."

Virginia just said, "God knew on the day I was born what day I was gonna die!"

"He does give you a brain though, Mom."

Whatever we do next, we believe God will be in charge of the entire project. Looking back, we believe that Michael became a part of our family because we stayed open to the opportunities God put before us. He had plans for Michael's life, and we just happened to be facilitators of that plan. We like to think of ourselves as merely the vessels He used to accomplish His purpose.

It's also crystal clear to us that we are supposed to use the success of *The Blind Side* to help others, and to pass on the sure knowledge we've acquired that each of us has the ability to make a difference. Our feelings are summed up by a saying of Billy Graham's, which Leigh Anne carries around on a card: "The legacy we leave is not just in our possessions, but in the quality of our lives. The greatest waste in all our earth, which can not be recycled or reclaimed, is our waste of the time that God has given us each day."

When *The Blind Side* premiered in Memphis, a gentleman who writes a society column attended the party afterward. He asked one of our friends, "Why do I not know these people?"

"There you go," they said. "You don't. That's just who they are."

We weren't black-tie people, they explained—Collins didn't have a debutante party. We only belonged to Chickasaw Country Club so Sean could play golf occasionally, and so we would have a nice place to eat brunch after church on Sundays.

"They don't do all those things," our friend said. "They don't go to the parties. You'll never see them at those things."

"Well, what do they do?"

"They have been helping kids in the public school system. That's what they do."

"Have they changed?"

"The only thing that's changed is that they can do more of it."

We couldn't have summed up our ambitions better. Cheerful giving is what we do, and we'd just like to do more of it.

✤

We continue to look for ways to give to other people's children, both within our Memphis circle and outside of it. Recently, we got a call from someone at Ole Miss soliciting a donation. When we hung up, it occurred to us that as much as we love to give to our alma mater, we've come to feel almost as passionate about public high schools. We find ourselves more and more interested in all kinds of grassroots giving, whether to schools, clubs, clinics, or church basement kitchens—anything that serves children who have less.

"You need to understand something," Leigh Anne tells people. "We're not as interested in helping good students, or comfortable students. We're interested in the kids on the absolute margins."

We have a different view of life now. Once Michael came into our lives our eyes were opened. We've seen hardship in this country that we refuse to look away from. Our family has come to understand how many children have desperate wants—and how little it takes to help fill them.

We get lots of letters and e-mails with stories about kids who are carving out opportunities for themselves from nothing, like wildflowers growing in a field. Not long ago we received a letter describing an extraordinary triumph at a school down in north Mississippi. Fourteen young women came out of nowhere to win a state championship in power lifting, an exercise in strength that involved a lot more than dead-lifting large dumbbells. They were competing in a relatively obscure sport and breaking gender barriers—yet they had just two or three uniforms to share between them. One of them would compete, come off the floor and change clothes, and then hand her uniform off to the next girl. It seems a minor gesture to give these kids some decent clothes to compete in—and while we're at it, to buy them championship rings.

One program close to our hearts is a Memphis youth basketball clinic run by our good friend Frank Harris. It was while playing for Frank's AAU team, the War Eagles, that S.J. got the nickname Spot. S.J. still works out with Frank sometimes on weekends and he has picked up some of his love for coaching. S.J. now does some youth coaching on his breaks from school, teaching five- and six-year-olds in a recreational league at the Independent Presbyterian Church. S.J. earns some money doing it, but the thing we like best about it is that it makes him get out of bed voluntarily. He's a champion sleeper, but he gets himself up at seven o'clock, and we don't have to wake him.

S.J. has been profoundly influenced by Frank, whose coaching philosophy is simple. The length of his practices are determined by "how much of the Holy Spirit got ahold of me."

Frank imbues kids with a sense of possibility, and inspires

them because of his own experience of turning bad situations into good. He came out of one of the toughest neighborhoods in Memphis, Binghampton, where he grew up one of ten kids in a two-bedroom house. "We thought we had it great, I didn't know how bad I had it," he says. "It was what I was used to." His father was a janitor, and his mother did laundry in a nursing home. Frank slept on a pallet in the living room with his brothers, and when anyone walked across the floor, they would joke, "Hey, you're walking on my bed." He was eighteen when he finally moved out into his own apartment, but he was so unaccustomed to being alone in a bed that he would put a pallet on the floor and sleep on it.

Frank contends that the biggest mistake we make as a society with our kids is that we don't believe in them enough. Too often we say, "That's too much for them to overcome." Frank knows from personal experience we can expect more from children. "You can teach kids to speak Chinese if you give it to them early enough," he says.

Frank uses basketball to teach ethics. He's got kids on the team from families so poor they won't have a Christmas, yet everything he coaches is all about giving. "The best thing in basketball is the pass," he says. Frank has such a giving heart that he is willing to help anyone with anything. A wonderful instance was when Sean fell behind at work as tax time approached one year. He was rushing to get all of his company W-2 forms out when Frank called. Frank could hear the panic in Sean's voice. He said, "We're coming to help." The next thing Sean knew the entire Harris family had formed an assembly line in his conference room and was stuffing envelopes. It was a beautiful sight.

Frank's motto for his teams is "When you give, you feel so much better than when you take." If he talks at all about winning, this is what he says: "Give God the glory and He gives us the victory."

❧

By March 2010 John Lee Hancock's inspirational little movie had grossed $250 million domestically and the number was still climbing. It had taken on a life of its own and just kept snowballing.

We were stunned by the enormity of its success—we couldn't figure out why everyone was so drawn to it. Then we realized the source of its power: the story of *The Blind Side* was inspiring not because Michael became a professional athlete, but because it suggested that we could all change people's lives *by investing time in individuals.*

The Blind Side is about the power of one. Ninety percent of the audiences watching the movie felt connected to it in some way. Similar things were happening in families and communities all across the country. We were in one of the worst economic periods of our generation, and yet all over America individuals were helping each other through hard times.

People gazed at the screen and saw themselves. Some could relate because they themselves were generous givers, and they said, "Hey, I've done something like that." Then there were those who felt they weren't doing enough, and who said, "Maybe I could give more." Finally, there were those who squirmed in their seats and said, "Why am I not doing my part?"

We hoped that everyone took the intentions they felt

when sitting in the movie theater or reading the book and put them into action. We hoped they went home, threw a dart at the phone book, and plugged into a cause, somewhere, somehow.

The Blind Side made problems seem smaller, and solutions to them more attainable. The title *The Blind Side* comes from the uniquely valuable role Michael plays on the field. At left tackle, he protects the quarterback's most vulnerable spot, his "blind side." We all have to protect each other better, individually. We don't have to throw money at a need to participate in alleviating it. Nor do we have to take on the entire problem of the public school system in this country by ourselves. Instead, we can make a difference in our own neighborhood and our own school system. We can help people right in our own backyard. We can look for ways to help on our street, at our church, or in our local grocery store.

We can go to the Boys and Girls Club. Or take a kid to a park and throw a ball. Or buy them a meal at Taco Bell. And while they're eating we can ask, "Hey, how's school going?" We can show up for a kid—and prove that we're not going away. More than anything, they just want to know we're coming back.

People often tell us, "I can't do a great, big thing like your family did." We always reply, "Okay, then do something small greatly." The thought of doing something may seem daunting. But don't let that stop you from taking the first steps. Our theory is that even if you only drop a dollar into the Salvation Army bucket, it's enough if it's given with a cheerful heart. You'd be amazed at what that dollar might do.

Take the story of Reed Sandridge. He is a thirty-six-year-old Washington, D.C., man who one day was suddenly inspired to give away ten dollars to a stranger. According to the *Washington Post*, Sandridge was working for a nonprofit organization when he got laid off in 2009. Rather than be discouraged, he walked the streets of the capital each day and looked for someone to give ten bucks to, because his mother had always told him, "When you're going through tough times, that's when you most need to give back."

Sandridge enjoyed giving away that ten-dollar bill so much that he decided to give away ten bucks *every* day, simply to spread a little generosity. It was harder than he thought—the next three people he offered the money to turned him down, skeptical of his motive. "What do I have to do?" one asked guardedly. Sandridge explained that he only wanted to foster a little kindness and care for others. He found doing something nice for people addictive—and he just wanted to spread the habit.

He carried a notebook with him and jotted down stories he heard from the people he gave money to. He gave ten dollars to someone playing the trumpet. He gave another ten to a busker dressed as the Statue of Liberty. He gave ten to a PhD and ten to a museum curator. He gave tens to some crazy people and to some homeless ones.

Sandridge began writing a blog about his experiences with the people he met: a woman on disability, an unemployed heavy machinery mechanic, a street drummer, a kid in need of new sneakers. Pretty soon strangers, inspired by his gesture, started stepping up to help the people he wrote about. His ten-spots seeded and sprouted and multiplied.

Reed Sandridge proves that even the smallest token of cheerful giving has a significant effect. Altruism is a renewable energy all its own; it produces a kind of chemical chain reaction. When we give to someone, we pass along not just cash, or an object, but the kind intention behind the gift. Which is then passed along in turn, triggering a cascade of successive giving.

The most marvelous effect of the movie was its contagion: audiences went to the movies to watch "real" people doing something for someone else, which they then thought about doing themselves. They seemed to come away from the theater saying to themselves, "There's no reason in the world we can't do something like that, too."

Cheerful giving has amazing power. You can share that power, too.

☙

We have no idea how many young Michael Ohers are on the streets of America, or out in the world. We just know that they are everywhere, kids of incalculable worth walking the streets of our cities, much too alone in the world. All they are asking for is love, and opportunity. They aren't asking for a Mercedes or a gold Rolex. They may not all be the next great professional football player—but they may be the person who grows up to cure cancer, or becomes a great husband or wife to someone.

There are a lot of intractable problems in the United States, but the problem of children in need is curable. We can all do something about it today, individually, through the smallest acts. We recently heard a remarkable statistic: if every church in the United States would see to it that just one child is adopted, the problem of homeless children in this country would disappear. If each of us got involved, we could wipe it out overnight.

When we *see* children—children who have previously been invisible—and see them not just with our eyes but with our hearts and in our souls, it's one of the most critical gifts we can give. If Michael, with all of his potential, could go missing, then how many other bright, wonderful kids are slipping through the cracks because people don't notice them?

"Hopefully people can take what they've seen from *The Blind Side* and reach out and help other kids in the inner city," Michael says. "I know tons of guys and girls who had more ability, more talent than I ever had, and who were smarter than me. But they didn't have anybody reach out and lend a hand."

As we write this, there are more than four hundred thousand American children in foster care. Roughly three hundred thousand children will be taken out of homes because of neglect and abuse in the next year, and one hundred thousand of those children will be available for adoption. Statistics show that if they don't get adopted, or cared for, over 70 percent of them will end up on the street or in jail, all because they don't have a family.

In our travels, we've met several people who have been in government childcare. Many of them are well over the age of twenty-one and, although they are adult working professionals, they still yearn for a family. Hardly one of them knows where they will be for Christmas or Thanksgiving. We recently met a twenty-seven-year-old woman who had "aged out" of the system. Nevertheless, she told us, "I still want to be adopted. People think just because I'm twenty-seven years old that I don't want to be adopted anymore. That's just not the case. I want a family. I want somebody to send me a birthday card. I want to know that someone, when they wake up in the morning, cares whether I'm alive or dead."

Government programs are great—we need a safety net. But the one thing government cannot do is look someone in the eye and say, "I love you, I want you in my home."

Of all the gifts we received from the story of *The Blind Side*, the greatest one we received was our sense of family. Not only did we get a son, we were all brought closer together. We've been through some trenches that a lot of other families don't go through. We came out of it with a stronger bond, and we're thankful.

If there is one meaning we'd like you to take from our story, it's this: the person you just walked past is the one who could change your life. So, every once in a while, stop and turn around. Find out about that person.

Eight years ago we didn't go out looking to adopt a child—a miracle simply hit us in the face and we didn't run from it. We can tell you from personal knowledge that the kid you never looked for can be the most surprising blessing in the world.

Not long ago, we heard the following story, which has become one of our favorites because it reflects our own experience. A couple that already had two teenaged children decided to adopt a six-year-old girl. One Sunday morning, the father got up and dressed for church and then went to rouse his children.

First, he went into his son's bedroom. The boy looked up from his pillows and said, "I'm still sleeping, Dad. Get out of my room." Next, the father went in to wake his elder daughter. She lifted her head from the pillows and said, "Dad, it's too early. Get out of my room."

Finally, he went into the third bedroom. His new little girl was already up. She had made her bed perfectly, and she was sitting on it, in her nicest dress, holding her doll. She was ready for church.

Maybe you never dreamed you'd adopt a child. But you might just get the child you always dreamed of.

It's hard to believe now, but S.J. was only seven years old when this all began. The other day S.J. was reminiscing about a family trip to Disney World. He said, "Michael, remember when we went there?"

Michael said, "S.J., I didn't go on that trip with ya'll. I wasn't around yet."

S.J. doesn't even remember life before Michael was part of the Tuohy family. He doesn't remember a time when Michael wasn't his brother.

Love, we've learned, can come into your life in a heartbeat. But the people who are your family aren't always the people who are blood related to you, and loving someone unconditionally is a lot easier than we make it out to be.

Give love and you will always get it back. That's our story, that's our message.

HOW YOU CAN HELP

We encourage you to become active in your own community and to discover the joy of cheerful giving for yourself. Go to our foundation's Web site, http://www.makingithappenfoundation.com, for more information about our favorite causes and projects, or to find links to other organizations that can help you explore the power of one. We challenge you to find a way to make a personal difference where you live and to donate to a worthy cause today.

Acknowledgments

It's a little surprising to become published authors, given our aversion to reading anything too long. For such an unlikely feat we owe deep thanks to a number of people.

First and foremost we credit the love, understanding, and personal contributions of our family—our three children, our parents, and the other members of the Tuohy and the Roberts families, as well as those in our extended family who share our lives with us.

Two men served as the main drivers of this project. Without Don Epstein and his staff at Greater Talent Network we would never have conceived of the book in the first place, or seen it through. Ed Victor has shepherded many wonderful volumes from idea to the page and we're honored to join the long list of his clients.

We are equally grateful to Steve Rubin and John Sterling at Henry Holt, who saw the possibilities and whose enthusiasm sustained us through the hard parts, and to everyone else at the publishing house who worked so hard to meet the deadlines.

We are also indebted to Esther Newberg of International Creative Management for bringing Sally Jenkins to the project and introducing us to a friend as well as a coauthor.

We thank the ever-cheerful office staff at RGT Management for keeping a tight ship and Carol Mattei for running Flair I Interiors like it's her own, which gave us the time to do this.

The Memphis Grizzlies have been exceedingly generous to Sean, allowing him freedom when he needed it and always encouraging him.

Lisa Cannon at Briarcrest takes such good care of S.J. and has never once reported us as bad parents.

Jimmy Young and our friends at Grace Evangelical Church lend us their constant prayers, advice, and support.

The Baltimore Ravens have made us feel like family.

We congratulate Houston Nutt for running the ball left, finally, and thank him and all our friends at Ole Miss for their support in all that we do.

Kitty Fox, in addition to being the most wonderful hairdresser in the world, is on call whenever needed.

We thank Jackie Bissley for helping us at every turn.

David Mortimer held our hands and made us look like we knew what we were doing.

We are more grateful to Miss Sue Mitchell than we can express.

We'd like to extend a broad thank-you to each and every person we have received a letter, e-mail, package, or phone call from. We have learned that people are givers by nature.

The story of our family would not have been widely known if not for our good friend Michael Lewis, whose bestseller *The*

Blind Side plunged us into this adventure. His wonderful work was an inspiration. We are also very thankful for the care shown by executive producers Gil Netter and Molly Smith, director-screenwriter John Lee Hancock, and the entire cast and crew of *The Blind Side* in transferring the book to screen with such emotional faithfulness, and to Warner Bros. for doing anything we've ever asked of them.

Finally, we thank God for all of our gifts, and for His guidance.

There is a scene in *Forrest Gump* when Tom Hanks is running across the country. Someone asks him, where are you going? He says, "I don't know, but I sure look forward to getting there."

We'll let you know when that happens.

ABOUT THE AUTHORS

LEIGH ANNE TUOHY grew up in Memphis and graduated from the University of Mississippi, where she met her future husband; she now owns an interior design company. SEAN TUOHY grew up in New Orleans and played professional basketball for a summer after college; he now owns more than seventy restaurant franchises. The Tuohys live in Memphis but travel all over the country speaking about their family, their faith, and how each of us can make a difference in the world.

SALLY JENKINS, an award-winning columnist for *The Washington Post*, is the author or coauthor of several books, including Lance Armstrong's *It's Not About the Bike* and *The State of Jones* (written with John Stauffer). She lives in New York City.

CPSIA information can be obtained at www.ICGtesting.com
Printed in the USA
LVOW07s2142260515

440025LV00004B/232/P